D0578012

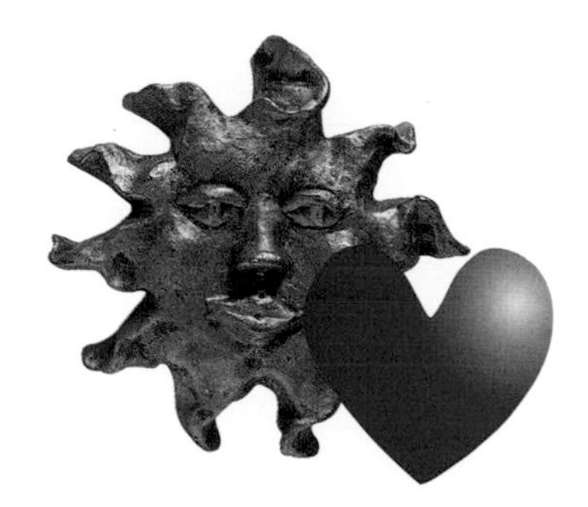

magic for lovers

magic for lovers

find your ideal partner through the power of magic

KATHLEEN McCORMACK

WITH AN INTRODUCTION BY BARBARA BIANCO

A QUARTO BOOK
First edition for the United States, Canada, and the Philippine Republic published in 2003 by Barron's Educational Series, Inc.

All inquiries should be addressed to:
Barron's Educational Series, Inc.
250 Wireless Boulevard
Hauppauge, NY 11788
http://www.barronseduc.com
International Standard Book Number 0-7641-5591-1
Library of Congress Catalog Card Number 2002106591

QUAR.MFL
Conceived, designed, and produced by
Quarto Publishing plc
The Old Brewery
6 Blundell Street
London N7 9BH
Project Editor Vicky Weber
Art Editor & Designer Sheila Volpe
Assistant Art Director Penny Cobb
Text Editors Pat Farrington, Alice Tyler
Photographer Will White
Illustrators Mark Duffin, Sally Launder, Ian Sidaway
Picture Research Image Select International
Indexer Diana Le Core
Art Director Moira Clinch
Publisher Piers Spence
Manufactured by Universal Graphics, Singapore
Printed by Leefung-Asco Printers Ltd, China

9 8 7 6 5 4 3 2 1

contents

INTRODUCTION

When we can't explain how something wonderful has happened, we use the word "magic." It describes an aspect of life both exciting and somewhat beyond our conscious control. We may not understand exactly how magic operates, but we can always recognize its presence in our lives. Magic makes everything appear bigger, brighter, and better.

Perhaps magic shows us the true nature of the universe. This expansive view is one that has been shared by lovers of all civilizations and cultures since the beginning of time. Not only does romance open our hearts, it expands our minds to see new possibilities. Love gives us the confidence and courage to act decisively. With our lovers beside us, we believe that we can accomplish anything, and the results of this outlook are astounding.

While our minds may not believe that we live in a magical universe, our hearts know the truth. All acts of love are magical in nature, regardless of the form they take. Works of poetry, music, dance, and painting are the magical children of our passions. Even the act of lovemaking transports us into a world beyond our imagination. Love dissolves all boundaries.

It could be said that magic is the art of making our intentions real. There is less of a distinction than we might think between acts of magic and everyday actions. In both situations we do whatever it takes to get the results we want. In magic we cooperate with the laws of energy to manifest our intent. In daily life we wrestle with the laws of physics until our desires are satisfied.

Performing magic is simply a matter of being aware of the creative process and putting on the hat of a creator. Each magical operation is performed in the mind, be it divination, invocation, or spell casting. The objects focus our thoughts and contact the forces involved. The rituals intensify and project our intent. Then the universe clothes our creation in matter. It's that easy.

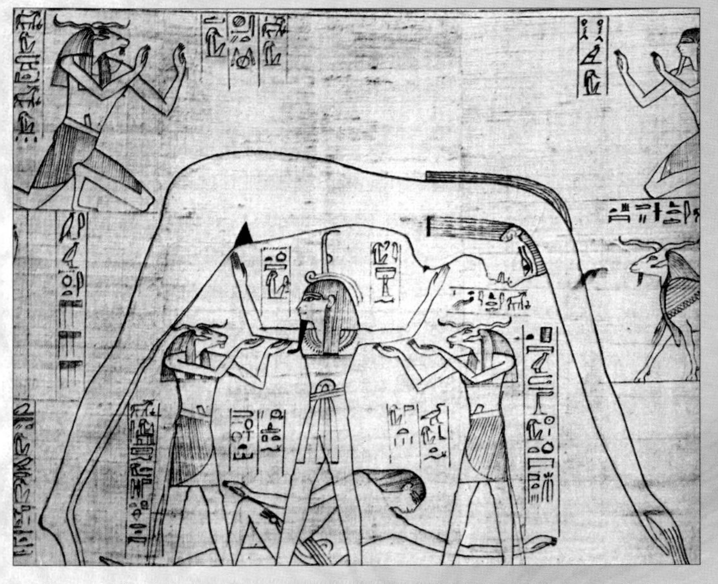

This funerary papyrus of Princess, Nesitanebtashru from circa 970 B.C. shows the Egyptian goddess, Nut, who was well known for her belief in and application to astrology.

This little book offers the secrets of magic to the lovers of the world. For some couples this knowledge will be the keys to the kingdom. In other cases making this information available could be inviting folk to play with fire. Keep in mind that the outcomes of magic, positive or negative, are determined by our intentions. The effects of our actions always return to us.

So what happens when we combine love and magic? With astrology we can discover which of our personal qualities are most attractive. We can look for our perfect lover among the 144 star-sign possibilities. The art of numerology will reveal the hidden motivations of a companion, guide us in the selection of a compatible mate, and help us recognize our dream house.

Just for fun we can communicate a secret message using flower symbolism, and look to the bottom of our teacups for signs of change. Along a more serious vein, the tarot cards can assist us in resolving relationship problems and our dreams can guide us in making decisions. If we dare we could try our hands at casting magical spells and creating protective talismans.

Whatever your motivation for picking up *Magic for Lovers*—whether it is to find entertainment or serious advice—these wise words will take you on a magical journey through the oracles that will encourage you to better appreciate life and its potential for love.

Barbara Bianco

CHAPTER 1

zodiac

Through the ages, astrology has exerted great influence on people from all walks of life. It has fascinated some of the most formidable intellects in history, while maintaining its appeal to the popular cultures of the day.

THE STARS

Find your lover in the stars

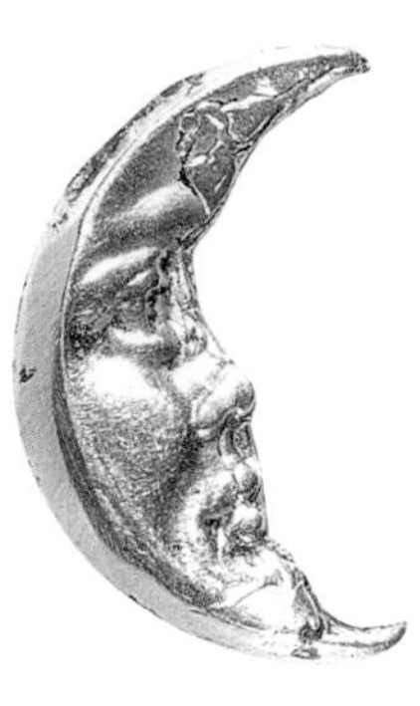

Our Star Signs provide important and intimate information about us. The briefest inquiry into astrology reveals the personal qualities that others might find attractive, as well as behaviors that could turn them away. The starry art teaches that every person has a number of gifts to give to the world. It also informs us that we have blind spots that we ourselves can't see, but that are obvious to everyone else. These shadowy areas are attitudes and habits that can be corrected. By applying the wisdom of the stars, we can become better people and better lovers.

Male or female, we have a love nature that is ours and ours alone. Men and women are different and that's certainly true where the Star Signs are concerned. For instance Aries guys and gals are not alike when it comes to love. Both are passionate, but the Aries man likes the chase, while the Aries woman prefers the possession. It's a fine distinction, but one that should be kept in mind, especially if you are an Aries or if you have fallen for one. Likewise there are subtle differences between the members of the opposite sex in all twelve Star Signs.

Let's not forget the chemistry of our love relationships. Without this magical element, there's no point in getting involved. With 144 Star Sign possibilities we can decide what is right for us. Each zodiac combination has advantages regarding the dynamics of romance. So what do you want? Is your dream to cuddle with your lover like a couch potato? Are you more interested in flaunting social convention? Do you feel the necessity to create a lifetime bond? Now you can look for the Star Sign combination that provides the ease, excitement, or stability that you desire.

Before we go any further, we should consider those unique individuals whose birth dates occur at the end of each Star Sign. Here the orb of the Sun spans the cusp of two zodiac signs and imparts a dual nature to anyone born at this time. For instance if your birthday is the twenty-first day of May, your personality will be composed of Taurus and Gemini qualities.

BELOW
Chinese zodiac figures from a late 18th-century Tibetan manuscript.

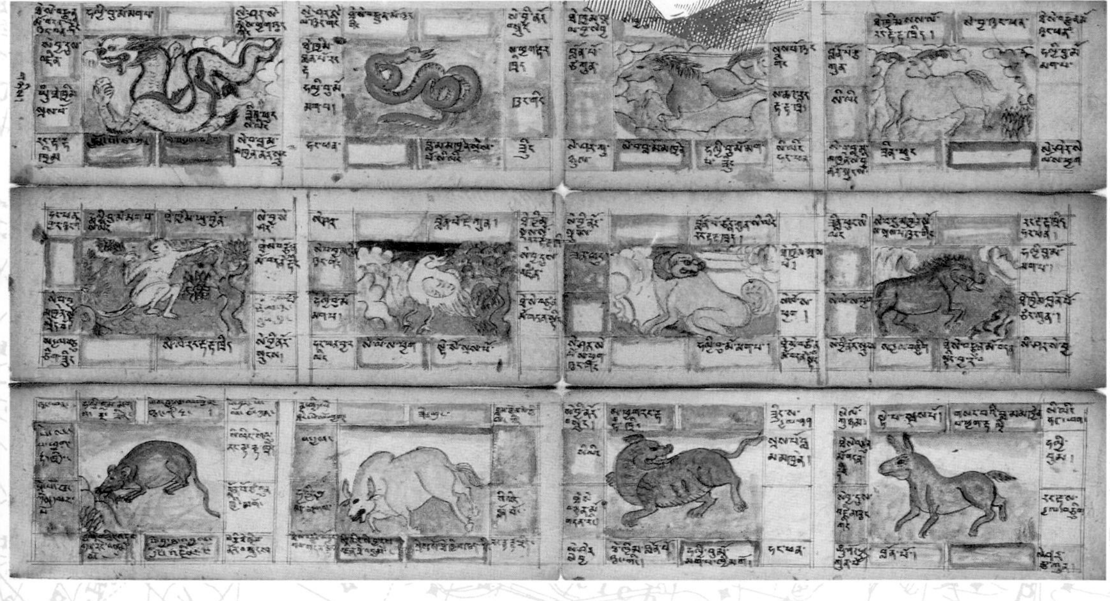

Ruling planet
Mars

Ruling symbol
The Ram

Ruling sign
Fire

aries *March 21 – April 21*

FIRST DECAN: If born between March 21 and 31, you tend to be very impulsive and have an explosive temper. You are also imbued with the idea of service to the community.

SECOND DECAN: If born between April 1 and 10, you are affectionate, steady, and faithful. You may appear malleable, but you will always get your way in the end.

THIRD DECAN: If born between April 11 and 21, you are the most typically Arian of the three. You alternate between highs and lows, are impetuous and loving, and will fight to the death for a friend or loved one.

MALE ARIAN

Challenge and variety are the cornerstones of this sign. To win this natural leader, you would have to let him do the chasing, and give him a balance of submission and independence. A clinging female would bore Aries sick. To an Arian, life is a series of conquests and all the world is his rival. He often makes alliances or is attracted to women who are already attached in some way. They seem to appeal to his desire to triumph over his adversaries, for Aries is a pirate at heart, and life is a succession of challenges and prizes to be won.

FEMALE ARIAN

Often blessed with a logical, direct type of mind, the female Arian finds herself working in fields like law, journalism, medicine, and architecture. The challenge of a strong uninterested male is sometimes enough to set her hunting. She has an enormous ego and belief that she is attractive and, often, through the sheer force of this self-belief, she can convince others that she is extra special. She is a loyal partner, acknowledging no fault, but expects you to share her every sorrow and joy. Like the male, though, her failing is that she wishes to possess you utterly but not be possessed herself.

Ruling planet
Venus

Ruling symbol
The Bull

Ruling sign
Earth

taurus *April 22 – May 21*

FIRST DECAN: If born between April 22 and 30, the stubborn and lazy elements in your character are often predominant. You can be more argumentative than the next two decans.

SECOND DECAN: If born between May 1 and 10, you have both discrimination and control. Your tendency to hoard could make your thriftiness seem like meanness.

THIRD DECAN: If born between May 11 and 21, you have an essential refinement. You are a reliable, stable, extremely generous, and thoroughly nice person.

MALE TAURUS

Practicality, honesty, simplicity, and conservatism sum up the main characteristics of the Taurean male. He is stubborn and persistent both in his courtship and in the general concerns of life. Basically loyal, he also hates to admit that he has made a mistaken choice, so that the Taurean often hangs on in a relationship that is injurious and even destructive. He is attracted to a feminine woman who would make a good mother, particularly one with a beautiful face and expressive hands. Ruled by Venus, the male Taurean is particularly attracted by beauty in any form, to the degree that a drab place or atmosphere will make him moody or depressed.

FEMALE TAURUS

Usually physically attractive with a lithe, sexy walk, a female Taurus carries an aura of motherliness and placidity under which a basic sensuality is barely concealed. She does not use her sex consciously as a weapon. In fact, there is a big element of giving comfort in this sexuality and a basic honesty in approach. She seeks security, both emotional and financial, idealizes beauty, respects success, and wants dependability. As a wife, this woman will never fail you, and your life will be secure and rooted in the things that have enduring values.

Ruling planet
Mercury

Ruling symbol
The Twins

Ruling sign
Air

gemini *May 21 – June 21*

FIRST DECAN: If born between May 22 and 31, you are a true Gemini in most respects. Your love of variety makes it difficult for you to achieve much while you are young. Later on, you will follow one of your interests to limited success.

SECOND DECAN: If born between June 1 and 10, your personality is better balanced than those of the first decan. You have a faculty for criticizing and analyzing that can be used profitably and you will achieve success and advancement.

THIRD DECAN: If born between June 11 and 21, you are the most sensitive and kind of this sign. Your only danger is that of being overly influenced by others and you can be led into extreme conduct through your desire to be popular.

Geminis are baffling, elusive, mercurial, restless, versatile, and always on the go. A better marriage risk as they reach their thirties, for they are at heart children who do not want to grow up.

MALE GEMINI

A male Gemini changes direction, so that he often ends up as jack of all trades. He loves to travel and lead an exciting life—boredom is like a little death to him. He is attracted to witty, intelligent women far more than to sex symbols, but cannot be bothered by a lengthy courtship. He is not so much promiscuous as restless, always seeking the novel and unexplored.

FEMALE GEMINI

Impulsive, variable, curious, adaptable, idealistic, the female Gemini is a mass of contradictions that make her a fascinating partner. Outwardly fun-loving, she has a serious side that longs for security and balance. She, like her male counterpart, can be in love with two people at the same time, loving them for different qualities. But if forced into a choice, she will pick the more secure type, provided he has as good a sense of humor as she has herself.

cancer *June 22 – July 23*

Ruling planet
The Moon

Ruling symbol
The Crab

Ruling sign
Water

FIRST DECAN: If born between June 22 and July 1, you are persistent in furthering your progress in life, you are gentle and overly sensitive, prone to jealousy and fits of depression and self-doubt.

SECOND DECAN: If born between July 2 and 12, you are among the strongest people of this sign. Usually possessing charm and poise, with strong physique and good looks, you have an appetite for life that sweeps all before it.

THIRD DECAN: If born between July 13 and 23, you are among the most pleasant of the Cancer group. You are gentle, sympathetic, kindhearted, and forgiving. You do not seem to achieve success when young.

Cancers are steady, sometimes bound by tradition, dependable home lovers, creative but not shy, and easily hurt. Like the crab, they are tenacious and, when in love, are determined and constant.

MALE CANCER

The male Cancer is often a one-woman man, who will not be interested in anyone except his ideal woman, although he has immense charm and his appeal to women is very strong. Often he marries late in life, because he wants happiness that will last.

FEMALE CANCER

Although the Cancer woman goes through adolescence dreamy eyed and idealistic, her practical home-making side takes over as she grows older and more conscious of money. She, like the male, demands the best of everything and this means men, too. Used to male attention, partly because of her deceptively fragile air, she usually presents a very glamorous yet soft appearance. However, feelings of insecurity and doubt make her vulnerable at times to criticism and rejection, and she will crave compliments and reassurance.

Ruling planet
The Sun

Ruling symbol
The Lion

Ruling sign
Fire

leo *July 24 – August 23*

FIRST DECAN: If born between July 24 and August 1, you are a faithful, honorable person who loves to mix with people and go to parties. Your only failing, if a female, is the love of personal adornment which can lead you into vanity and extravagance.
SECOND DECAN: If born between August 2 and 12, you are extremely ambitious and have loads of confidence. Your faults, if carried to extremes, would be your penchant for bossing others and your outspokenness.
THIRD DECAN: If born between August 13 and 23, these are the impulsive, impatient people who sometimes give up the struggle when things become difficult. They are affectionate, generous, and kind.

MALE LEO

The Leo man must always be the center of attention, both in love and in life—he will brook no rivals. He is the royal sign of the zodiac and with this go all the attributes of honor, pride, warmth, passion, tenderness, and also, conversely, love of luxury and a destructive jealousy. The Leo man wants to rule, but hates an easy conquest. Challenge is the spice of life to him.

FEMALE LEO

The Leo woman is not quite as basic and simple as the Leo man. She is inclined to be snobbish, only because she demands the best and knows what she wants. If you can't put her there, then bow out of the race. She has a very solid appreciation of money and will often combine a highly paid career with marriage. Her energy is such that, if she becomes bored, she could become destructive either to herself or to others, so for her own sake, she feels it is better to develop and channel her talents.

virgo *August 24 – September 23*

Ruling planet
Mercury

Ruling symbol
The Virgin

Ruling sign
Earth

FIRST DECAN: If born between August 24 and September 3, you like to be alone and do everything after due consideration. Marriage would be difficult for you, unless you had a measure of freedom or isolation at times.

SECOND DECAN: If born between September 3 and 13, you are the most successful Virgo, for your progress will be due to your thoroughness, critical faculties, and reasoning powers. Your persistence in the face of obstacles will win the day.

THIRD DECAN: If born between September 13 and 23, you are the type who could occasionally indulge in a rather lurid but secret love life. You are firm in all other respects, but possibly because of this, feel the need to break out sometimes.

MALE VIRGO

Virgos are the hardest of all signs to get to know. The Virgo man is an enigma, sometimes to himself. He seems to be very much a loner and intrigues other signs because he shows a surface warmth and sparkle yet clearly, underneath, is alone and aloof. One type will have lots of short, meaningless relationships that touch him only lightly; the other type will develop a relationship first from friendship through to romance and will, if the partner is suitable, marry her after a long, gradual courtship.

FEMALE VIRGO

The Virgo woman is fascinated by the reasons and motives behind the actions of others. She likes to talk and to feel she is of help to others. However, she never really listens, mainly because her mind has already completed what the other person is going to say. She is a great organizer, so your lives will run to plan. However, if you take her for granted, she could end your association and you would then be faced with your life in chaos and the knowledge that you have lost an intriguing and charismatic woman.

libra *September 24 – October 23*

Ruling planet
Venus

Ruling symbol
The Scales

Ruling sign
Air

FIRST DECAN: If born between September 24 and October 3, you are the more practical Libran. Music will play a big part in your life. You are less lazy than the other decans.

SECOND DECAN: If born between October 4 and 13, you could easily become too preoccupied with material possessions. This is the artistic decan, which gives great charm and loads of talent, but also the ability to discard people when the going becomes tough.

THIRD DECAN: If born between October 13 and 23, you have the concept of service and the love of people. You are gregarious and you love reading, pleasure, and alcohol, and tend to put yourself last so you become a doormat for your loved ones.

Libra is the sign of beauty, harmony, and love. All Librans are good dancers and most are unusually attractive. Often, because of their particular way of seeing both sides, they will argue for the underdog, even if they themselves don't approve.

MALE LIBRA

The Libra man likes soft, appealing women and dislikes arguments. He really enjoys intelligent discussion on an abstract level, so he has to see that the intellectual companionship and rapport between you is lasting before he commits himself.

FEMALE LIBRA

The Libra female can be flirtatious, loves parties, people, drinking, and dancing. She finds it hard to express her innermost thoughts and worries. As lies are abhorrent to her, she usually endures the shocking hurtful break-up of an idealized love affair before she learns to look below the surface. When she does choose happily, the man is a lucky man indeed. He has a partner in the true sense of the word.

scorpio *October 24 – November 23*

Ruling planets
Mars & Pluto

Ruling symbols
The Eagle & Scorpion

Ruling sign
Water

FIRST DECAN: If born between October 24 and November 2, you are rather detached and can sometimes seem to be on another planet. You are restrained and modest and, rather surprisingly, are easily influenced by others.

SECOND DECAN: If born between November 3 and 12, you are the sunny-natured Scorpio, often blunt and tactless, but also friendly and open. However, you tend to trust friends a little too easily as you judge them by your own standards.

THIRD DECAN: If born between November 13 and 23, you are the strongest of the Scorpios. You are a bundle of energy whose ambitions know no bounds and whose persistence and intelligence will eventually bring you what you want.

This is the most inflammable sign of the zodiac: the unforgettable people. Proud, vain, usually either good-looking or intriguing, with an air of command, like Leos, they never take a back seat.

MALE SCORPIO

The Scorpio man does everything intensely. He runs risks in his kind of fierce sport, such as mountaineering. Challenge is the operative word for a Scorpio man. He is intense with an aura of violence around him. He could not marry a female Scorpio as this all-consuming love might destroy him. He is more attracted, as a lasting relationship, to a calmer, saner partner.

FEMALE SCORPIO

The Scorpio woman is passionate but selective, self-assured and poised, dignified, and restrained (unless her famous temper gets out of control), and she draws people to her like a magnet. Her passions are strong; if she finds a man, it can be to the exclusion of everything else. This possession can become a little frightening and smothering, for she is concentrated on her man and can turn her back on the outside world.

Ruling planet
Jupiter

Ruling symbol
The Archer

Ruling sign
Fire

sagittarius *November 23 – December 21*

FIRST DECAN: If born between November 23 and December 1, you are a rebel. You love analyzing and dissecting things and are bluntly honest and sometimes offensive because of this. You should always try to work for yourself.

SECOND DECAN: If born between December 2 and 11, you are so open you find it hard to deceive or keep a secret. You are emotional and very independent. Discussions, particularly on philosophical or occult subjects, fascinate you.

THIRD DECAN: If born between December 12 and 21, you would be more concerned with humanitarian issues and could seem to be detached and indifferent. Often you are single-minded in your search for personal fulfillment and material success.

MALE SAGITTARIUS

The Sagittarian male is, from the female point of view, the most satisfying and the most exasperating sign of the Zodiac. He makes a wonderful lover and friend, is warm, demonstrative, uninhibited, highly principled, and sometimes romantic. But, when he wants to, he can also be extremely difficult and then the other side of his nature comes into play: his unconventionality, allied to devastating honesty, his great willingness to sacrifice everything for freedom of thought and action and his hatred of domination.

FEMALE SAGITTARIUS

She is self-sufficient, sometimes too independent, free, generous, talkative, intelligent, aware, and has no desire to compete with a man, or to cling possessively. The man she chooses must have physical appeal, for she is herself a warm, passionate woman, but there must also be something for her to respect and admire about him, something interesting or alive about his work. The sense of being supported by someone who thinks as she does and cares, really cares, is the cornerstone of her marriage.

capricorn *December 22 – January 20*

Ruling planet
Saturn

Ruling symbol
The Goat

Ruling sign
Earth

FIRST DECAN: If you were born between December 22 and January 1, you can be fickle at times. This is because you are indecisive and go on to something new before you have completed the project at hand.

SECOND DECAN: If born between January 2 and 11, you are extremely stubborn. You are not possessed with as much energy as the rest of your sign, but you are a conscientious and steady worker. Musicians are often born in this decan.

THIRD DECAN: If born between January 12 and 20, you are the leader type, with brains, determination, and ambition. You are friendly and modest, but you have one failing, that of sometimes not seeing the forest for the trees.

MALE CAPRICORN

If your lover is a Capricorn, then you will have a challenge on your hands to retain the love of this dedicated climber. He is loving, but unable to show affection easily. He is always conscious of dignity, ambitious for money and position, and never likely to admit defeat; however, this star type can improve with age. He always brings stability and sometimes luxury to his marriage, which gives due consideration to prestige, power, and wealth.

FEMALE CAPRICORN

The Capricorn female needs a lot of encouragement, even though her façade seems self-sufficient and sophisticated. She is, in reality, self-contained and shy. Definitely interested in worldly success, the Capricorn woman is an ambitious perfectionist who is interested in serious matters. You will have no difficulty in getting your Capricorn woman to marry you once you have shown her that you are willing to depend on her to keep your life stable.

Ruling planet
Uranus

Ruling symbol
The Waterbearer

Ruling sign
Air

aquarius *January 21 – February 19*

FIRST DECAN: If born between January 21 and 31, you are highly intelligent, you practice more self-discipline than the other decans, and your kindness springs from the heart. Religion means a lot to you.

SECOND DECAN: If born between February 1 and 10, you tend to miss opportunities either because you are dreaming of future glories or you are suspicious of people or circumstances. You tend to be stubborn and impatient.

THIRD DECAN: If born between February 11 and 19, you are intuitive and can penetrate to the heart of human nature. You are highly artistic and have great concentration. You do everything well and cannot suffer fools or bores.

MALE AQUARIUS

Freedom is the central feature of the Aquarian male's character. Lively, rebellious, and unconventional, the Aquarian is an idealistic and persuasive reformer. His wry sense of humor, candor, and honesty are his most appealing traits, while a fine mind, original approach to life, and exciting personality make him a dangerously attractive but very risky marriage partner.

FEMALE AQUARIUS

The Aquarian woman is interested in the occult and astrology. She is a wonderful dancer. She dresses in an individualistic style, but is always at the height of fashion. Spontaneity appeals to her and freedom is very important. Once you have learned to understand her, your marriage to the Aquarian female could be exciting, rewarding, and ideal companionship in later years, provided you share some of the same interests.

pisces *February 20 – March 20*

Ruling planet
Neptune

Ruling symbol
The Fishes

Ruling sign
Water

FIRST DECAN: If born between February 20 and March 1, you are ambitious and crave recognition and appreciation, but you hold back and are very cautious at times. You love entertaining people.

SECOND DECAN: If born between March 2 and 10, you could sometimes live in a sea of trouble, on your own little island. Because of your predilection for domestic upheaval around yourself, you can achieve little in life until you are over forty.

THIRD DECAN: If born between March 11 and 20, you are too impractical at times, but have great self-confidence, and can analyze a problem and get to the heart of the matter through logic. You are restless and love travel, particularly on the water.

MALE PISCES

Like Gemini, Pisces have a dual nature. This sign is two fishes swimming in opposite directions and, indeed, Pisces can be both dreamy and fiery. Sympathetic and soft-hearted, imaginative and compassionate, a Pisces can sometimes be too loving and generous for his own good. He is oddly secretive, living with an unworldly attitude toward material success, but if you are loved by a Pisces man, you have tasted the nectar of the gods!

FEMALE PISCES

The Pisces woman is even more vulnerable than her male counterpart. She has her own picture of what love should be and, if you do not live up to that picture, she will feel betrayed and bereft, and could become bitter or unbalanced. Always looking for someone to live for, someone to belong to, someone to revolve around, this girl is trusting, romantic, and very feminine. She is sympathetic and intuitive, making a fine partner for the right man who will relish her attention and devotion and protect her with his life.

It's happened! You've found someone you click with. It's clear from the emotional chemistry that he or she enjoys your company. Like Romeo and Juliet, the physical attraction leads you to believe that your relationship is destined. But then you wonder how long it will last.

ARE YOUR STAR SIGNS COMPATIBLE?

Improve your chances of a happy life and love

This is a legitimate concern and one for which astrology has good advice. Over time, a great deal of wisdom has been gained from studying the various star-sign combinations. There is a supposition that two sincere people can make any relationship work if they give it their all. Still, some zodiac combinations are easier to navigate than others. And if you've chosen a difficult combination, you'll appreciate the warning that you are heading into rough waters.

EMOTIONAL CHEMISTRY

Use the following charts to gauge the chemistry of your relationship. First locate the section containing your star sign, then read down the column until you find the sign in question. You may love the results, you might hate them; but whatever the outcome, at least you are prepared.

aries

Aries with Aries

A surprisingly compatible union, if all others factors are satisfactory.

Aries with Aquarius

There would be the interest of pioneering new ideas, but there would be little peace.

Aries with Pisces

There is the constant attraction of opposites, but the Arian would always consider the Pisces to be slow and dreamy, and would never understand them fully.

Aries with Taurus

Not a successful combination, given the two strong, stubborn signs together.

Aries with Gemini

If the Aries is a female, this combination could succeed.

Aries with Cancer

Aries could easily annihilate Cancer in this relationship.

Aries with Leo

If the male is Arian, this combination would be bound to be successful.

Aries with Virgo

This combination could work, if the male is Aries and there is an intellectual closeness and a similarity of interests.

Aries with Libra

These opposites could have a magnetic attraction—or repulsion!

Aries with Scorpio

There would be competitiveness in this combination, as these two signs have a lot in common and are both demanding and ruthless.

Aries with Sagittarius

The best combination of all, provided both parties were strongly individual.

Aries with Capricorn

Two strong, inflexible signs, so there would be not be much give-and-take.

taurus

Taurus with Taurus
Too steady to be interesting, yet this combination could achieve prosperity.

Taurus with Aquarius
The Aquarian would be too casual about material things and too impersonal in the affairs of the heart to make Taurus happy.

Taurus with Pisces
There will be little intellectual attraction between these two, but affection and friendship could be strong.

Taurus with Aries
This could only succeed if the woman were the Taurean partner.

Taurus with Gemini
Rarely a successful combination.

Taurus with Cancer
There would be few high spots in this association; it would be quiet and serene.

Taurus with Leo
Physically this could be a great union and, if both partners are down-to-earth and straightforward people, it could be a happy marriage.

Taurus with Virgo
Sexy, this could be a wonderful partnership. However, if the Virgoan were not strongly physical, Taurus would in time be repelled by the coldness of his partner.

Taurus with Libra
If the Taurean were the breadwinner, then this could be a wonderful combination.

Taurus with Scorpio
There would have to be a lot of common ground and mutual trust before this would work.

Taurus with Sagittarius
A difficult combination, but opposites attract. The sex drive would be strong.

Taurus with Capricorn
This union would be best for two people who are home-loving and earthy.

gemini

Gemini with Gemini

This combination would never be static and would probably not last.

Gemini with Aquarius

An exciting, adventurous existence, and a great intellectual attraction and physical bond.

Gemini with Pisces

This could be a good partnership, particularly for mutual creativity.

Gemini with Aries

This union would need to develop outside interests in common.

Gemini with Taurus

A difficult combination—but if the Gemini is a male, he could get a lot of help and support from his practical, levelheaded Taurus partner.

Gemini with Cancer

This union would entail a lot of tolerance, work, and sacrifice to make it a success.

Gemini with Leo

In a partner, Geminis look above all for understanding and sympathy. Leo—vain, jealous, and egocentric—would find it hard to take second place.

Gemini with Virgo

This could only be successful in the short-term.

Gemini with Libra

A good pairing—very compatible.

Gemini with Scorpio

These signs are so different. The union might be undermined by Gemini's love of freedom and Scorpio's jealousy.

Gemini with Sagittarius

A good partnership—each is adaptable and tolerant, likes freedom and intellectual and physical activity.

Gemini with Capricorn

These two would not appreciate each other's qualities.

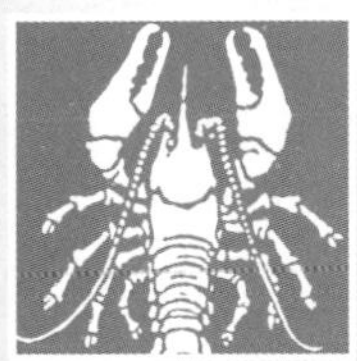

cancer

Cancer with Cancer
This union would be a very quiet one. However, if both had the same goals in life, they would pull together.

Cancer with Aquarius
The Cancer's need to cling would in time tire and bore the Aquarian.

Cancer with Pisces
Emotionally, this combination has much in common. However, practical objectives and everyday living could become confused and lack planning.

Cancer with Aries
Aries could easily annihilate Cancer in this relationship. It would not be a good combination for permanency.

Cancer with Taurus
A very successful union, although it could be a little unadventurous.

Cancer with Gemini
If the Cancer is female, there is a better chance of this union succeeding.

Cancer with Leo
In strong, extrovert Leo, Cancer subjects should find an ideal partner.

Cancer with Virgo
This could be a successful combination because Cancer is slow and sure, so he would appreciate the dedication and perfection of the Virgo nature.

Cancer with Libra
This would be a difficult union in many ways. Cancer's emotionalism could easily offend the finely-balanced Libra.

Cancer with Scorpio
This could be a good union: there would be a strong intuitive tie here.

Cancer with Sagittarius
This relationship would provide a very close friendship at the best.

Cancer with Capricorn
Opposites often attract and this could be a good combination.

leo

Leo with Leo

The battle for supremacy could destroy both—go for friendship.

Leo with Aquarius

The very different attitudes could interest both, but there would be little understanding of each other.

Leo with Pisces

A puzzle for both parties. Leo could be intrigued; and Pisces attracted to the straightforward approach of Leo.

Leo with Aries

A Leo would find an Arian provides the necessary drive, but the Arian's need for flattery would not be met.

Leo with Taurus

This is a better combination if the male is the Leo. Good for material wealth.

Leo with Gemini

This could be a strong combination.

Leo with Cancer

This is a good combination—particularly if the male is a Leo as he would have an admiring audience.

Leo with Virgo

There would be little chance of this union being a success due to the lack of common aims.

Leo with Libra

Libra's inherent good taste and balance could be offended by the extravagance of Leo's character and his conceit.

Leo with Scorpio

Another wonderful union, but Scorpio hasn't the tolerance of Sagittarius.

Leo with Sagittarius

This could be a great combination, if Sagittarius thinks Leo's vanity is endearing.

Leo with Capricorn

Both signs are out for position and power, but have different methods of seeking them, so this union is unlikely to work well.

virgo

Virgo with Virgo

A splendid match. The only problem would be the tendency to nag.

Virgo with Aquarius

This would be a purely intellectual relationship. Aquarius would prove a puzzle to Virgo and Virgo would depress Aquarius.

Virgo with Pisces

Virgo is analytical and logical, while Pisces is the opposite, so not much hope here.

Virgo with Aries

A moody combination which could conceivably work, but only if Aries were older, male, and tolerant.

Virgo with Taurus

If the male is Virgo and the female Taurus, this could be a very happy match.

Virgo with Gemini

An unlikely combination: Virgo might well stifle Gemini.

Virgo with Cancer

This would work best if the Virgo is male, but Cancer could feel shut out.

Virgo with Leo

This is not usually a successful partnership unless both partners have similar backgrounds, attitudes, and aims.

Virgo with Libra

Virgo's set ways would rile Libra, although both signs are perfectionists.

Virgo with Scorpio

This could really be a shattering experience, particularly to the Virgoan.

Virgo with Sagittarius

These two are so different, it would depend on the tolerance of the Sagittarian to be successful.

Virgo with Capricorn

A down-to-earth conservative union which should succeed because neither is too emotional. Each partner must be tolerant of the other's failings.

libra

Libra with Libra

Both would be too intent on avoiding arguments and not hurting the other's feelings to really relax and live.

Libra with Aquarius

A harmonious and exciting relationship.

Libra with Pisces

A happy mixture, but they should spend a lot of time getting to know each other before marriage so as to avoid disillusionment.

Libra with Aries

Opposites attract. Libra could be hurt badly in this combination.

Libra with Taurus

The only problem here would be if the dreamy Libran is the breadwinner.

Libra with Gemini

A good union. Librans could soothe Geminis and give them the balance they lack.

Libra with Cancer

These signs do not have the same attitudes or aims. They would confuse each other.

Libra with Leo

An excellent combination; Libras share Leo's enthusiasm but could restrain their impetuosity and show Leos the other side of the coin.

Libra with Virgo

Perfectionists both, this could be a rewarding union, but only if Virgos can curb their criticism.

Libra with Scorpio

If Libra could stand the tempestuousness of Scorpio, this would be a great partnership.

Libra with Sagittarius

An excellent prospect.

Libra with Capricorn

These two often seem sent to discipline each other and, provided they are philosophically inclined, this could be quite successful.

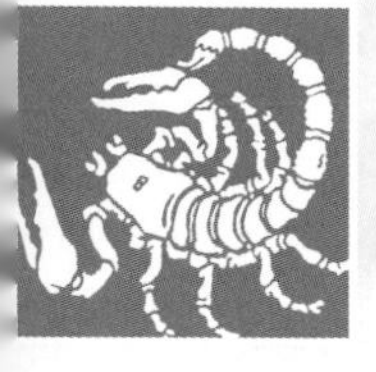

scorpio

Scorpio with Scorpio
An emotionally wearing association, excellent physically, but only workable if both have exactly the same aims.

Scorpio with Aquarius
This would only be successful for a short while unless there is trust and tolerance.

Scorpio with Pisces
This is a terrific combination when the male is Scorpio.

Scorpio with Aries
Not a good combination. Too much ruthlessness, love of power, and fire.

Scorpio with Taurus
A physical relationship mainly, this combination would only work with lots of mutual trust and tolerance.

Scorpio with Gemini
Not a very satisfactory relationship because of the intensity and passion of Scorpio.

Scorpio with Cancer
A very good combination, but an emotionally-based one that would have little to do with reason or communication.

Scorpio with Leo
If there is mutual tolerance and co-operation these two signs could almost move the earth, but only if both sides are mature.

Scorpio with Virgo
The result of this pairing could be surprising.

Scorpio with Libra
The Libra would have to the giver and extremely tolerant for this union to work.

Scorpio with Sagittarius
A possible combination but only if Scorpio learns to curb his jealousy.

Scorpio with Capricorn
This combination could be extremely good. It would all depend upon whether both parties pulled together toward some common goal.

sagittarius

Sagittarius with Sagittarius
Could be a winner. Lots of enthusiasm and communication.

Sagittarius with Aquarius
This could be a very good combination, sparking off mental interests.

Sagittarius with Pisces
This is a doubtful combination. Neither would appreciate the other's viewpoint.

Sagittarius with Aries
This is a winning ticket! Both signs complement and see things to admire and respect in each other. They can go a long way together.

Sagittarius with Taurus
A strongly physical union but a difficult one which only time might cement.

Sagittarius with Gemini
A more mental than physical union, this would require a lot of adjustment to enable it to work.

Sagittarius with Cancer
This could be a very successful match if the male is Sagittarian and great care is taken not to hurt Cancer's feelings by too much blunt truth telling.

Sagittarius with Leo
This could work well if both signs show tolerance toward one another.

Sagittarius with Virgo
A difficult union—better if the Sagittarian is the male partner, since Virgo's organization mania could depress the happy-go-lucky, untidy Sagittarius.

Sagittarius with Libra
An excellent union. Both are interested in people, are idealistic, and affectionate.

Sagittarius with Scorpio
A very interesting union, but an explosive one.

Sagittarius with Capricorn
This is one of the most difficult combinations of all, as there seems to be nothing in common, nothing either would like or admire in the other.

capricorn

Capricorn with Capricorn

This could be a dull, serious combination, with a tendency for both partners to use others.

Capricorn with Aquarius

This would not be an easy partnership because both signs are ruled by Saturn.

Capricorn with Pisces

This could be a very productive union, despite the fact that these signs are as different as chalk and cheese.

Capricorn with Aries

If both subjects are mature, this could be a rewarding union, but the Capricorn will not be dominated, so the Arian partner would have to adapt to make this a success.

Capricorn with Taurus

A productive union with an abundance of worldly success and relatively few clashes.

Capricorn with Gemini

This would be the attraction of opposites—successful if both partners are mature or tolerant—or if the Gemini is the male partner.

Capricorn with Cancer

If the man is a Capricorn, this could be a combination giving peace, harmony, productiveness, plenty, and long-lasting love.

Capricorn with Leo

Two headstrong signs—each thinking their way is best.

Capricorn with Virgo

This combination could make a successful partnership, resulting in prestige, power, and mutual understanding, particularly if the female is Virgo.

Capricorn with Libra

Not usually considered to be a harmonious duo.

Capricorn with Scorpio

This is a good combination, but common goals would be essential for it to succeed.

Capricorn with Sagittarius

A difficult combination with plenty of fireworks, but a lot of mutual respect.

aquarius

Aquarius with Aquarius

This combination could mean that nothing would ever be achieved.

Aquarius with Pisces

There would be great mutual attraction here, but also bewilderment and perplexity.

Aquarius with Aries

The Aquarian would hate to feel he is possessed and dominated.

Aquarius with Taurus

These two signs are on different wavelengths.

Aquarius with Gemini

This combination would be exciting. Each would spur the other to new achievements and successes—and interest would never lag.

Aquarius with Cancer

This can be a harmonious association, but usually only if the female is the Cancer.

Aquarius with Leo

A wonderful physical union, and if both are tolerant and prepared to give, it could be a wonderful combination.

Aquarius with Virgo

These two signs do not seem to generate great passion, but for a marriage where the partners run a business together, there would be nothing to beat it.

Aquarius with Libra

A lovely, heady combination with all the attributes of a lifelong love affair.

Aquarius with Scorpio

The Scorpio partner may turn out to be too strong, fiery, and dominating.

Aquarius with Sagittarius

This could be a risk, but is also one of the best combinations for Aquarius, provided the Aquarian could learn to say "I'm sorry" and the Sagittarian understand there are other points of view.

Aquarius with Capricorn

Capricorn would tend to be restrictive and possessive, while the Aquarian disregard of established tradition could enrage the Capricorn.

pisces

Pisces with Pisces

A dreamy, cloud nine duo that would need lots of cash and practical help in life.

Pisces with Aquarius

This is the meeting of minds, but the Pisces might become too submerged and irritate the Aquarian.

Pisces with Aries

These two signs have very little in common. Aries always feels Pisces is indecisive.

Pisces with Taurus

There would be little intellectual attraction between these two, but friendship could be strong.

Pisces with Gemini

Although one will be a constant mystery to the other, these two signs could agree to disagree. There could be basic differences due to Pisces' lack of logic.

Pisces with Cancer

This could be a lifetime partnership, although there will have to be one leader.

Pisces with Leo

This combination could succeed, particularly if the female is Pisces, as she will admire the drive, honesty, and strength of Leo.

Pisces with Virgo

This is the attraction of opposites and could only last if both types are tolerant.

Pisces with Libra

If neither is overly ambitious or highly gifted artistically, this combination would be very happy, idealistic, and emotional.

Pisces with Scorpio

There is a wonderful attraction between these two signs.

Pisces with Sagittarius

A doubtful union, depending on the main interests of the Sagittarian.

Pisces with Capricorn

If the Piscean is a woman, this combination could be rewarding.

CHAPTER 2

numbers

The magic of numbers has been appreciated for thousands of years—since the time of the ancient Egyptians at least. Pythagoras, the ancient Greek mathematician, believed that numbers are the essence of everything, including love.

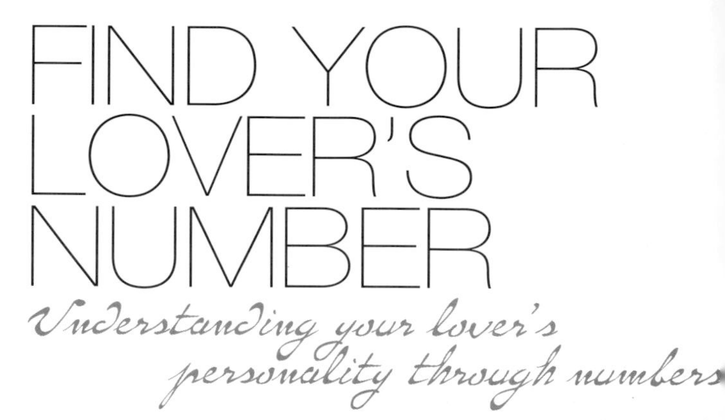

FIND YOUR LOVER'S NUMBER

Understanding your lover's personality through numbers

Has anyone ever said to you "I've got your number?" It's a popular expression meaning that this person understands the true motivation behind your actions. More often than not, he or she is correct and has come to this conclusion intuitively.

You don't have to be psychic to figure out your lover's motivation. You can use numerology to peer into the depths of your beloved's nature. In the same way, your lover can discover what makes your heart skip a beat.

WHAT'S YOUR MOTIVATION?

The Primary Number shows your personal motivation. It is determined by adding up the numbers in your birth date.

Example: September 30, 1971

Step One: 9 + 3 + 0 + 1 + 9 + 7+ 1 = 30

Step Two: 3 + 0 = 3

Result: the Primary Number is 3

THE MEANING OF PRIMARY NUMBERS

The ancients claimed that each number has an esoteric significance. This deeper meaning is created by the principles of sacred geometry. Likewise your Primary Number reveals the mechanical workings of your inner nature. While this number is yours for life, it's your decision to use the prime energy in a positive or negative way.

1 ♥ THE MONAD

The Unity of the Monad is the symbol of the deity, the oneness of divine purpose, the hub of the universe, the Parent of the World, and the Sun. Considered to be a masculine number, because of the tradition that the male was created first, those who came under the influence of this number will show the following characteristics: great tenacity, singleness of purpose, self reliance, great achievement, concentration, ingenuity, genius (occasionally), love of action, and strength. People controlled by Number One will be leaders, will welcome responsibility, will be kind to those weaker than themselves, and will be friendly and considerate. But they will also tend to underestimate the character and work of others; and they will be stubborn, brash, and overconfident, scorning good advice, insisting on haughty independence, and lapsing into conceit, narrow mindedness, bigotry, and intolerance.

The Duad

The Duad is considered to be a feminine number and, with its two sides, is balanced and harmonious. It represents diversity, justice, and equality. Those who come under its influence will show consideration to others, placidity, and a hatred of tyranny and all forms of selfishness. They have many friends because of their understanding and considerate nature. However, if their traits are taken to the extreme, they can be too passive. Their distaste for strife could lead to the shirking of all responsibilities while the ability to see both sides of a question can make their nature fatalistic and sometimes even indifferent. They need the strength of Number One.

3 The Ternary

In ancient civilizations this was believed to be the perfect number. It is considered to be a male number and has been linked with many diverse ideas over the centuries, including the Christian Trinity and the god of the ancient Greeks. Those who come under this number are confident, creative, and fun, with specific traits like enthusiasm, fortitude, optimism, and adaptability. They will generally be successful people because of their business acumen, organizational flair, and persuasive charm. However, all these traits can become negative if taken to excess. They can be overconfident, indifferent, impatient, and lacking in purpose.

THE TETRAD

According to the ancient Greeks, the Tetrad is the root of all things, as Zeus, the King of Gods, has four letters in his name. The Number Four represents the four winds, the points of the compass, earth, wind, water, and fire. It is also supposed to represent truth. Its symbol is the square, which stands for reality and solidity. Hence Number Four people are stolid, strong willed, loyal, honest, conventional, and hardworking; however, they might rebel against too many rules and regulations. They always see the good in others and do not judge them. But they lack imagination and can get stuck in a rut and, therefore, overvalue routine. They need Number Three people to inspire and innovate them to achieve success.

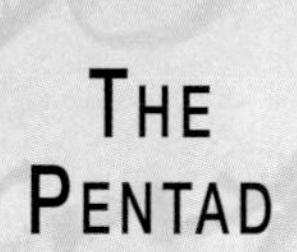

THE PENTAD

The Quincunx or the Pentad was regarded by all the ancients as the symbol of health and fecundity, while to the Egyptians alone it also signified prosperity. It was universally linked with marriage and propagation. Those who come under the influence of this number will show vivacity and versatility, courage and a strong physical constitution, romantic ardor, friendship, empathy, and the ability to find pleasure in the little things in life. They love to travel and to explore the unknown and are cosmopolitan in their outlook, being able to mix easily with all strata of society. Their affections are seldom deeply engaged, so they make better friends than lovers. They can be irresponsible and lacking in concentration, and act on impulse. They are often seen to be unreliable but this is usually due to thoughtlessness and to the fact that they try to do too much at once. They need the steadying influence of Number Two, who could counteract their faults.

THE HEXAD

The Hexad is represented by a six-sided figure. It is considered one of the happiest numbers because it represents harmony and completion. Those coming under its influence will show idealism, smooth harmony, strict honesty, kindness, and care for the sick and lesser abled. They are never selfish, intolerant, or self-indulgent, and do not esteem money for its own sake but as a means of benefiting others. They are faithful, loving spouses, and good parents. They have few unfavorable qualities, although their idealism, if carried to excess, can make them appear superior, and their lack of concern with material success may well affect their families. Often they will not stand up for their rights and will assume an air of martyrdom; they can also be too soft and kindhearted and allow people to impose upon them.

7

THE SEPTAD

The Septenary or Septad. This is the most mysterious and interesting of the Primary Numbers. The Pythagoreans considered it to be sacred because it was the highest Primary Number. The Septad may be said to represent the qualities of wisdom, balance and completion, evolution, and endurance. Those who come under the influence of this number will show self-discipline, fortitude, spiritual strength, solitude, love of knowledge, love of privacy, intuition, occult power, and great intellectual activity. They will be ahead of their time in their philosophy and beliefs, will love knowledge and value it above everything. Their very love of solitude can be their undoing, as they hate being forced to mix with people and can become overly critical. They should learn the true worth of friendship to avoid becoming lonely in old age.

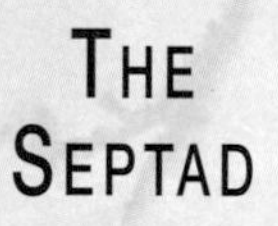

♥

The Ogdoad

The Ogdoad was greatly revered in Egypt, as it was believed that eight souls were saved from the flood in Noah's Ark. Number Eight signifies balance, reality, and strength. Those who come under the influence of this number will be extremely practical and will show organizing ability and business sense. They have all the qualities of Number Four people but in greater measure. They might not fall passionately in love, but they can give a lifetime of loyalty and steady affection. Their lack of imagination can make them blunt at times, and they can annoy others by their refusal to concede that there may be dimensions other than the practical. A Number Five person could help them achieve their potential.

9

♥

The Ennead

The Ennead was thought by many of the ancients to be perfection, harmony, and completely limitless. The Romans considered this a special number. Those who come under this number show perfectionism, discretion, great intellect, understanding, a leaning toward logic, philosophy, fine arts, and martial pursuits. They are equipped with brilliant minds. They are kind and willing to help others succeed. Their thoughts and actions are ruled by honesty and consideration for others. They make fine, sympathetic friends and do not seem to judge others or feel superior to them. This is the number of genius, like Number One, but they lack the driving power of the Monad. The detrimental qualities of Number Six belong to these people too. They may set too much store on knowledge for knowledge's sake, and may be lethargic and dreamy. These people need to learn self-discipline and concentration, and to value the natural gifts they have been given.

LOVE BY NUMBERS

The Heart and Love Match Numbers

Are your chances for deep and abiding love determined by numbers? You might not think so, but numerologists believe that the name you are given at birth contains many deep secrets. Some of these mysteries pertain to your ability to love and relate to others. For those who know the code, the combinations of various letters in your name can release an enormous amount of information.

Numerologists are as systematic in their work as accountants, their counterparts in the business world. They calculate the frequency of the various numbers, noting those which are abundant and those which are absent. They carefully consider the occurrence of consonants and vowels. All their findings are cataloged neatly in charts. This examination is known as a numerological analysis.

The final outcome is a number or a set of numerical values representing the vibrational constitution of a particular human personality. Everything in creation vibrates by its own distinctive tone. A numerological reading helps you to understand how you can make a personal contribution to this evolving universe.

In terms of love, this world is a puzzling place. You are told that—at a spiritual level—all beings are created equal, but if you focus on the physical form, it is easy to forget that fact. It's an unfortunate fact that we tend to notice the differences rather than the similarities between individuals. Differences separate us while similarities bring us together. Why not focus on the positive aspects of life and love? Through this study of numerology you can learn a lot about compatibility and making the most of yourself—and your lover.

The sum of the numbers in your name reveals the vibrational expression of your whole being. It is called your Heart Number and can give you an insight into that side of your personality that is responsible for your capacity to love and form relationships.

FIND YOUR HEART NUMBER

...and learn about yourself

No one of us is perfect, so this number shows you where to make an effort. It reveals the talents you can develop and the limitations that you should be aware of so that you can allow yourself to be loved for your whole self.

It is very simple to calculate your Heart Number. All you need to do is use the table below to work out the sum of the letters in your birth name. When you have reduced them to a single digit, look through the descriptions on the next few pages to learn a little more about your loving self.

Example

Marion Lane: 4 + 1+ 9 + 9 + 6 + 5 + 3 + 1 + 5 + 5 = 48

4 + 8 = 12

1 + 2 = 3

So, Marion Lane's Heart Number is 3. Marion would now turn to page 50 to find out what her Heart Number means for her.

Dreams can come true!

Single letters

1	2	3	4	5	6	7	8	9
a	b	c	d	e	f	g	h	i
j	k	l	m	n	o	p	q	r
s	t	u	v	w	x	y	z	

HEART NUMBERS

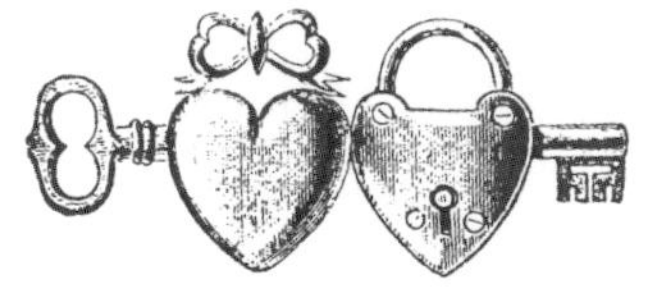

1 This number is the number of romance and yet you need an attraction that is intellectually based. Marriages could be brought about suddenly, and meetings could take place while you are traveling away from home or in a place of learning. You should exercise caution in married life as boredom could lead to extramarital affairs.

2 This number is discriminating in its choice of a marriage partner, mainly because the love of comfort and stability is foremost. You will demand a person with a good mind, but one who is eminently practical and able to provide the financial security you desire.

3 You are idealistic and long for partnership in marriage, but your spirit of sacrifice can be abused. If you let your intuition take over, your choice will be unerring, for you understand people's motives very well and will usually pick someone whose interests match with yours, making a very companionable life.

4 You are attracted strongly to marriage by your emotional and affectionate nature, but your choice can lead you into difficulties. You desire an active and dominant partner and yet there is a part of your character that hates being hurried or dominated. You may find the way is made tricky for you by the envy and spite of others.

5 You marry for life and have a loving and happy partnership because you are sincere and honorable, but curiously there is often a history of broken, pre-marital romances through your partner's insincerity. Companionship is vital to you. Religion and philosophy play a large part in your life.

6 Usually a late developer, you might be shy and unable to express yourself easily, although you are ardent underneath. Paradoxically, you have periods of rash behavior owing to inner impatience. Your marriage is most likely to be successful if you marry after the age of thirty-three.

7 You are often designated a flirt. This is not so, although you should not marry in your teens before your real character and taste are molded. Once married you are a true and loyal partner. You are so intellectually and physically active that you tend to meet far more people than most of the other numbers.

8 This number brings travel, change, and variety. You may have more than one marriage due to your innate restlessness and love of change. The happiest marriage for you would be with an older person when you yourself are over thirty. You could run a business with your marriage partner.

9 Marriage is your gateway to the fulfilled life, and to this end you bend all your thoughts, hopes, and wishes. Care should be taken to make sure that your aims and motivations are commensurate with your partner's, as failure of one to keep up with the other could cause frustration.

It is very interesting to work out and understand your Heart Number, but in terms of love, it will have most resonance when looked at in combination with your lover or potential lover's Heart Number. Use the Table of Harmonies to do just this. Work out your lover's Heart Number, go to your Heart Number box on this page, look at the combination of your two numbers—make an informed choice.

THE TABLE OF HARMONIES

Your love match—or mismatch

Remember that compatibility means different things to different people. Some people prefer a lover with qualities similar to their own. Others may relish the challenge of relating to someone entirely different. The loving choice is yours.

KEY: If a number vibrates to another, it means the attraction is strong and mutual.

If the number attracts another number, the two people are compatible.

When the number opposes another, there would have to be a constant measure of diplomacy to prevent the union from foundering.

If a number is merely passive to another, there are no outstanding influences connected with this union, either fortunate or unfortunate.

1

Number One
Vibrates to: 9
Attracts: 4, 8
Opposed to: 6, 7
Passive to: 2, 3, 5

2

Number Two
Vibrates to: 8
Attracts: 7, 9, 1
Opposed to: 5
Passive to: 3, 4, 6

3

Number Three
Vibrates to: 7
Attracts: 5, 6, 9
Opposed to: 4, 8
Passive to: 1, 2

Number Four
Vibrates to: 6
Attracts: 1, 8
Opposed to: 5
Passive to: 2, 7, 9, 3

Number Five
Vibrates to: another 5
Attracts: 3, 9, 2
Opposed to: 4
Passive to: 1, 6, 7, 8

Number Six
Vibrates to: 4, 2
Attracts: 3, 9
Mildly opposed to: 1, 8
Deeply opposed to: 5
Passive to: 7

Number Seven
Vibrates to: 3, 5
Attracts: 2, 6
Opposed to: 1, 9
Passive to: 4, 8

Number Eight
Vibrates to: 2, 5
Attracts: 1, 4
Opposed to: 3, 6
Passive to: 7, 9

Number Nine
Vibrates to: 1
Attracts: 2, 3, 6
Passive to: 4, 5, 8

You've found the right person, and the two of you are going to live happily ever after. Or so you think! Did you know that the wrong address could spoil this fairy tale ending?

YOUR DREAM HOUSE NUMBER

An auspicious address?

The address of a house reveals the type of vibrations that will be encountered there. The energy of your immediate surroundings can cause your relationship to bloom vigorously or wither on the vine. Numerology will confirm if you and your lover are living in the right place.

SHARING SPACE

Let's say that you and your sweetie reside at 5445 Rose Tree Road. You begin by adding up the individual digits of the house number. If your house has only a name, convert the letters into numbers using the chart on page 46.

Example: 5445 Rose Tree Road

Step One: 5 + 4 + 4 + 5 = 18

Step Two: 1 + 8 = 9

Result: This address is a Number Nine house

A Number Nine house is not for everyone. It's a charming place but it always needs upkeep. If you and your lover have high-powered careers, this home is best left to those who have the time to nurse it and its renovations along. Instead you might select a Number One address.

A Number One house is streamlined and modern in its design. It would be a great setting for entertaining and showing off your success. This type of residence would serve your daily needs and support your dreams as a couple.

By comparing your House Number with your Primary Number, you can determine the level of domestic bliss that you can experience at any address. It may be necessary to play around with the figures until you find the perfect space to share.

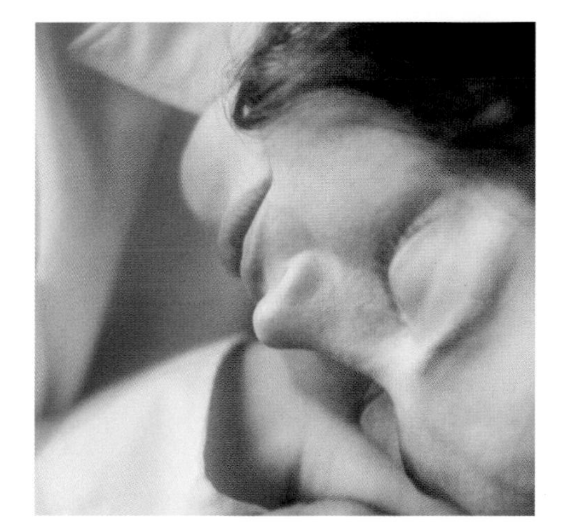

Lucky period
February to April

The Number One House

The vibration of this house is predominantly one of leadership. The house usually contains one dominant, independent personality. If there are two such people, it causes difficulties. So partners need to compromise for the sake of peace in the house. This house number suits careerists and can be exciting without monotonous routine. It is often the home of a creative person and/or a self-employed one. It is usually uncluttered with strong colors and should have many books and modern appliances. There is often a strong sense of leadership which if unchecked can develop into a superiority complex. Sometimes the house can be lacking in warmth, so it is important for there to be flowers, music, and at least one pet.

The Number Two House

The vibration of this house is predominantly one of partnership, cooperation, and duality. This should be a very popular place bursting with visitors but not en masse. The house will usually look immaculate from the outside, though perhaps a little run-down and untidy inside. It might be seen to have a lived-in feel. The occupants of the house should be careful to get things done rather than being overly conscious of what other people think of them. Under this number, people always crave affection and encouragement, so sometimes they will have other lovers. However, these will be short-lived as loyalty is of great importance to those under the influence of the Number Two house. There is an almost childlike quality to the house and so it would suit those who are young at heart.

Lucky period
Summer

The Number Three House

The vibrations of this number give the house a positive, optimistic, and exciting atmosphere. The décor should be unusual with artistic flair and use of bold colors. It usually houses entertaining people who sparkle with optimism and warmth. They tend to attract people to them because of this and because of their heightened sense of empathy. They are original thinkers who try many new things and, because of this, they can be disorganized and often cannot finish what they start. These kinds of people find it hard to settle as they crave freedom. Young people may be escapist and older people may have been through several marriages. Accepting responsibility is often quite difficult for them and they can become manipulative if they do not seem to be getting their own way. Ideally, they should work with other people to prevent them from becoming bored and frustrated.

Lucky period
Summer

The Number Four House

The vibrations of this house number are honesty, practicality, and tenacity. These houses tend to be well-built, well-designed, and professionally finished with many useful design features. The owners are usually good at DIY. However, sometimes they have an over-inflated opinion of their skills, so wiring and other areas that really do require a professional should be carefully examined if you are buying. Families would suit this house and guests would always be welcome, as long as the parents do not become snobbish and dictatorial. This can easily happen and usually one partner dominates the other, leading to tension and even separation. If this is guarded against, it can be a very happy house.

The Number Five House

The Number Five vibrations are happiness, versatility, and a nurturing nest for talent. This house suits those who love people and adventure. However, care should be taken not to make them feel restrained. They can be overwhelming and insensitive at times. Although they abhor all routine, they can motivate others and achieve success as long as they fully intellectually engage with their work. The house is typically spacious with expensive furniture and green/blue décor. To ensure spiritual well-being, the house should also have some white walls.

The Number Six House

The Number Six vibrations are harmonious, with emphasis on tolerance, social responsibility, and a love of humanity. The house tends to be a warm and comfortable refuge for those who need help, and the house is always full of love. Those in need are protected at all costs and this sometimes places undue strain on the occupants, especially financially. There is never really a shortage of material goods, as these seem to arrive when needed, more often than not as gifts, but material rewards are not sought by the owners. Harmony makes this a good house number for relationships as long as both partners have an intellectual affinity, shared goals, similar idealism, and a healthy sex life. This is because of the very strong desire for the physical and if these attributes are not present in the relationship, it can lead to insecurity and even violent jealousy.

The Number Seven House

The Number Seven vibrations are hard work, wisdom, independence, and spirituality. This house can give the illusion of taste and wealth through clever décor. The house suits pets, especially cats. The inhabitants of this house can seem aloof, but this is just shyness, particularly in large groups.

The house has to have a quiet corner in which the inhabitants can escape the world and other people. It is essential for their health that they can recharge their batteries in this way. They usually have only found stability through hard-learned personal trials and, if this is not found, then they might prefer not to live in the real world. This can make partnerships difficult. However, with a positive mental attitude they can make a significant mark on the world through their inner wisdom, spiritual strength, and natural healing and psychic abilities.

Lucky period
Mid-season

The Number Eight House

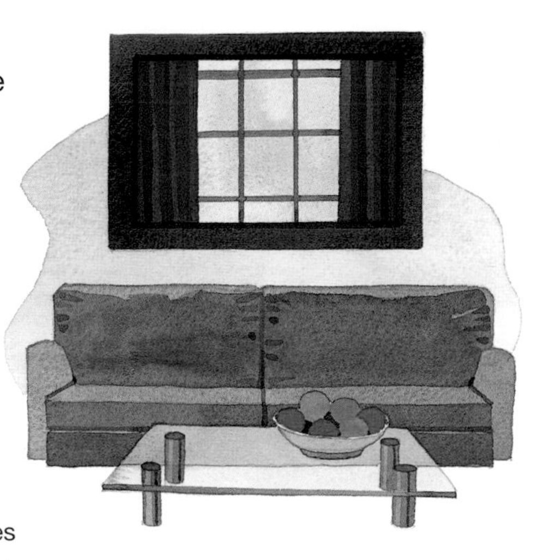

The Number Eight house exudes power, potential, prosperity, and permanence. This house has an aura of confidence and daring, along with the financial stability to back it up. The décor is usually luxurious, neat, and supremely comfortable. It suits richly-colored drapes, pale-leather sofas, glass, and an area for study. The inhabitants are very independent, sometimes extremely inconsiderate, and are used to being obeyed. This can lead to problems in a partnership, such as constant arguing. However, when both partners are happy and successful, it can be a good nurturing environment.

Lucky period
July and August

The Number Nine House

The Number Nine vibrations are compassion, sensitivity, benevolence, and artistry. This dwelling is usually shabby but beautiful, full of unique gifts and curios. This house should be full of reading material from all sources. This is the magnetic center for a loving, caring, and sharing individual or family. All inhabitants are artistic in some respect. If they are not artistic, then they lean toward the caring professions, such as doctors or teachers where helping others is a priority. This is not a household for those who like their finances in a healthy, organized state, but there is always room for a guest or friend. The inhabitants of the house will be much happier later on in life when they can concentrate more on themselves and they can be found exploring far-flung corners of the world.

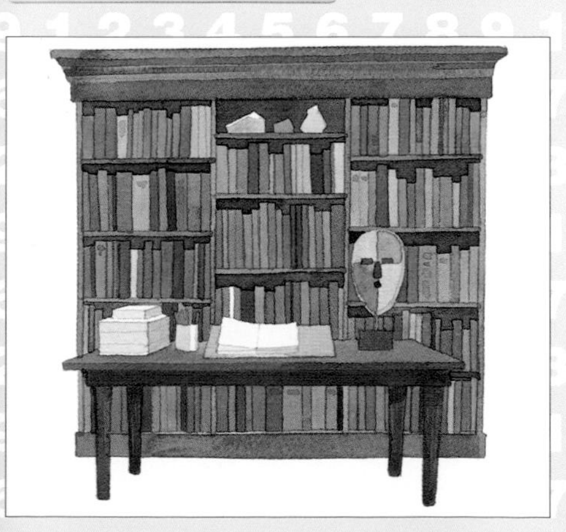

CHAPTER 3

tarot

There are seventy-eight cards in the tarot pack: twenty-two Major Arcana and fifty-six Minor Arcana.

The Major Arcana are the twenty-two picture cards: the cards containing strong prototypal symbols and meanings, for example, The Lovers and Strength.

The fifty-six Minor Arcana are split into four suits—Cups, Coins, Swords, and Staves—each containing fourteen cards. There is one extra court card, the Knave, which was dropped from our modern pack of playing cards in the sixteenth century. The cards of the Minor Arcana are illustrated in a literal manner with, for example, the Four of Swords shown as four swords.

LOVE IS ON THE CARDS

Using tarot to foretell love

Tarot is so profound in scope, you could apply the cards to any area of your life. But for now, focus only on the cards most closely associated with love.

Experience has shown that the best advice for lovers comes primarily from the twenty-two cards of the Major Arcana, the sixteen court cards, and the fourteen cards of the suit of Cups.

In a tarot reading, we play the part of the Enquirer, if we are seeking advice. If we are interpreting the cards, we assume the role of the Reader. A tarot reading begins as the Enquirer selects a court card to represent his or her question. Then Reader shuffles the cards and spreads them on the table. Finally the Reader explains each card regarding its magical meaning and its place in the overall pattern.

When we ask the tarot a question about love, we receive a love story. We are shown the romantic drama that is being played out in our lives. We can look back to see the reasons for the situation. We can reflect on how we are responding to the situation. We can look forward to how the situation will work itself out. Must the events in the cards take place? No, any outcome can be altered by a change of heart.

The art of reading involves linking the cards to give a meaningful interpretation.

A CARD TO REPRESENT THE ENQUIRER

Before laying the cards out in a reading position called a Spread, you, the Reader, must choose a card appropriate in age and physical type to represent the Enquirer, the person requiring the reading. This card must be chosen from court cards of all suits.

The four court cards within each suit (the King, the Queen, the Knight, and the Knave), apart from having their own separate meanings, represent people of differing ages and physical types. There are twelve male court cards in the tarot pack and only four female cards, so we cannot set an age for the Queens, but the male ages are:

The King
Thirty-five and over

The Knave
Infancy to eighteen (these can sometimes be female)

The Knight
Eighteen to thirty-five

Sometimes, but not often, an overly serious young man can turn up in the cards as a King, and a "Peter Pan" type older man can be portrayed as a Knight.

Having chosen the court card, you must decide on the Enquirer's suit. You must note the skin, eyes, and hair of the Enquirer in that order; the determining factor being the tone of their skin.

If a person's hair has whitened with age, they will drop one tone, so that with the exception of Coins, the fairest (who will stay as Coins), Swords become Staves, Staves become Cups, and Cups become Coins.

Staves *stand for people with light olive skin, brown, hazel or green eyes, and dark brown to light brown hair.*

Coins *have the same color eyes as Cups people, but with blond, white, or red hair.*

Swords *stand for people with black or dark olive skin, black or brown eyes, and black or brown hair.*

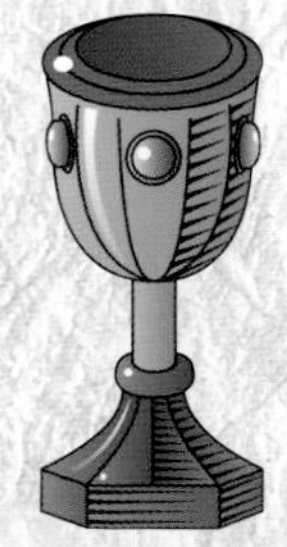

Cups *stand for fair complexioned people, with blue, gray, hazel, or green eyes, and blond or light-brown hair.*

The Cup Suit

The King of Cups – *The Husband*

This card represents a fair-complexioned, light-eyed, brown-haired man over thirty-five years of age. If with another King, it means it is a professional man.

The Queen of Cups – *The Wife*

This card represents a fair-complexioned, light-eyed, brown-haired woman. It also means a happy marriage or that the Enquirer is a good social mixer.

The Knight of Cups – *The Proposal*

This card represents a fair-complexioned, light-eyed, brown-haired man from eighteen to thirty-five, usually a bachelor. This card can also mean a proposal or invitation.

The Knave of Cups – *The News Bringer*

This card represents a fair-complexioned youth or child of either sex. It also means the birth of a child, the start of something new, or new methods in business.

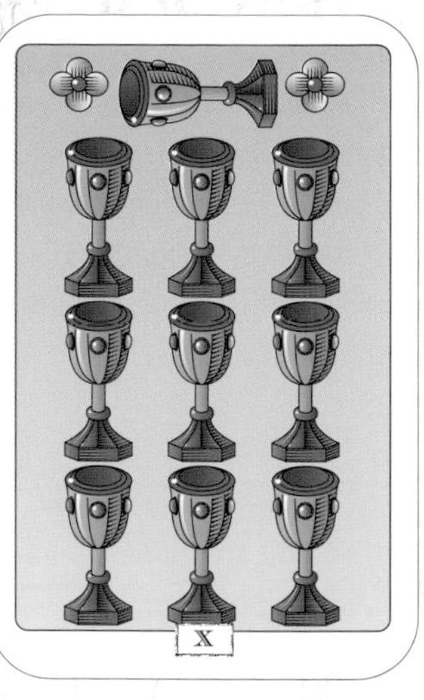

Ten of Cups – *Fame and Prestige*

This stands for public esteem, even fame, and the respect of friends. It also shows that the Enquirer has or will do work for the public that has brought or will bring happiness and acclaim. It also denotes a happy and secure domestic circle in the house or the hometown of the Enquirer.

Nine of Cups – *The Wish*

This card represents many aspects. These are fame, success, emotional security, good luck, good health, and sudden and unexpected gifts or gain from loved ones. If placed near negative cards ("badly placed") it cannot lose its strength, but its benefits will be delayed through the Enquirer's own negativity or wrong thinking.

The Eight of Cups – *New and Happy Horizons*

This card denotes new experiences such as new friends and interests. It can also mean saying goodbye to an unhappy past. This card, combined with other love cards (the Lovers, the Two, the Nine, or the Ace), can mean a marriage. In other respects, it can mean rewards for past actions, a small journey, a pleasure trip, and sometimes a new home. If badly placed, it means the Enquirer must make a positive decision to end a frustrating situation.

The Seven of Cups – *The Multi-Talented Dreamer*

This card means that a sudden stroke of luck will happen to the Enquirer and benefit artistic endeavor or something recently started. It represents mental activity and creative talent, but the correct choice will have to be made in order to succeed. If negatively placed, it denotes an unrealistic, impractical dreamer. It can also mean that a wrong choice will be made through self-deception or indecision.

The Six of Cups – *Our End is in our Beginnings*

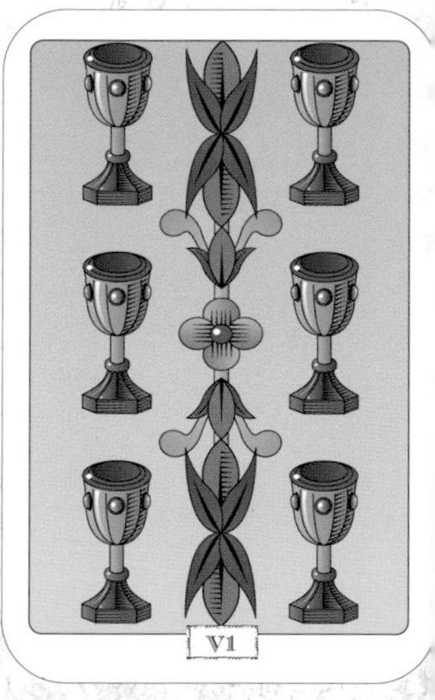

This card represents either the family or the relevant past. It can mean that old friends will come back into the Enquirer's life, be an indication of the cutting of past ties, or that a dream from the past will now be realized. If badly placed, it means that the Enquirer tends to live too much in the past or that the Enquirer is dominated by the family and is perhaps frightened to break away.

The Five of Cups – *The Crossroads of Life*

This is the card of something gained, like inheritance, but always with the thought of something regretted or lost. This card denotes the crossroads—a decision has to be made, and new alternatives should be explored. If badly placed, it means that love has been lost. It can also mean that the Enquirer suffers from a lack of confidence.

The Four of Cups – *The Divine Discontent*

This card signifies a state of dissatisfaction that is always the forerunner of change and improvement. It can sometimes, if coming near a court card, mean that outside interference will change the course of a love affair. If badly placed, it can signify that the Enquirer's own discontented attitude to life will mar a future change of circumstances.

The Three of Cups – *Hopes Fulfilled*

This is a happy card denoting the joyous conclusion of an emotional matter. It can also mean fame and success in any artistic endeavor in which the emotions are called into play. It can also mean a happy wedding celebration if near the marriage cards (the Lovers of the Major Arcana, the Ace, the Two, or the Nine).

The Two of Cups – *Engagement*

This is the card of loving unions, alliances, and the signing of papers or contracts. In terms of love, it means friendship, companionship, and reconciliation after a parting. If badly placed, it can mean that difficulties will arise in the partnership.

The Ace of Cups – *Marriage*

The marriage card, like all the other aces, stands for new beginnings in the emotional sense. It symbolizes creative talent that brings warmth, pleasure, and talent to others, especially in a new undertaking. It can also denote spiritual inspiration, or a loving, giving nature.

The Major Arcana

1. The Magician – *Commencement*

This card symbolizes quick action, mental activity, and articulacy, as well as occult power. It stands for initiative, willpower, self-awareness, decisiveness, and learning in all areas. Decisions made will result in triumph, even when those decisions are risky. In a negative aspect, it denotes trickery, uncertainty, or using and abusing occult power for selfish ends.

2. The High Priestess – *Healing and Spiritual Awareness*

This cards stands for divination, creative talent, and a thirst for learning, especially unusual or difficult subjects. It often denotes a healer or a teacher. It also means religious conviction, and it implies intuition or psychic power. It can also represent those involved with the written word, for example, publishing, as well as those who deal with the visually beautiful.

3. The Empress – *The Horn of Plenty*

The Empress represents abundance, fertility, motherhood, and a blossoming of emotional and intuitive feeling. In terms of the home, it represents domestic harmony, stability, and increased prosperity. It denotes good health, a generous and happy spirit, and a force for good. In relation to others, it can symbolize a benefactor or a wealthy marriage.

4. The Emperor – *Majesty and Might*

This card, as opposed to the intuition of the Empress, stands for logic and the triumph of intelligence over passion. It represents a leader who has energy, knowledge through experience, stability, wealth, and great influence. It can denote a government or official, a multinational corporation, and the United States of America. When next to Justice, it can mean a politician.

5. The Hierophant – *The Public View*

This can mean the desire for ritualistic religion or society's approval. It can also mean the discovery of secrets. It denotes a scientific or religious person, or the realization of a late vocation. It is the inspirational card of the performing arts, and can denote any occupation that serves the public.

6. The Lovers – *Emotional Choice*

The meaning of this card is always underlaid by a choice or the freedom of choice. It symbolizes the emotional relationships of life such as a love affair or idealistic friendship. It can denote a moral choice that will or has caused suffering, and, sometimes, means a flash of insight that resolves a moral problem.

7. The Chariot – *Well-earned Triumph*

This card means triumph through personal sustained effort and victory through control; it is never inherited success. It can mean greatness, particularly in creative work. It also means triumph over difficulties, over ill health, and over poverty, which will bring wealth and honor. It also denotes the conquering of your enemies, as long as they are truly your enemies. It can also mean unexpected news by word of mouth, or sometimes travel in luxurious conditions. Only when coupled with the Tower or Death is this card to be considered negative, when it could be read as the collapse of a plan.

8. Strength – *Right is Might*

This card is the strongest in the tarot and influences all the others, lessening any negative influence. This is the spiritual world overcoming the material one. It denotes integrity, and means that the Enquirer's own moral strength will overcome all difficulties. This card can be seen as a mastery of life in its most positive aspect and illustrates the Enquirer's willpower, self-discipline, endurance, and tolerance. On a more mundane level, a wonderful opportunity will arise which, if the Enquirer has the courage to grasp it, will lead to great happiness.

9. The Hermit – *Divine Guidance by the Inner Light*

This card is the card of slow careful progress leading to success. It is sometimes a warning that prudence and careful planning are needed or that the inner voice should be listened to more often. It can simply mean that the Enquirer will be given advice or guidance, sometimes legal, which will be of benefit. It can mean a prospective long journey or the yearning for travel. If negatively placed, it can denote excess timidity in delaying events or that the Enquirer has refused to face adult responsibilities. It can also mean a delay caused by his or her procrastination.

10. The Wheel of Fortune – *Karmic Reward and Luck*

The Wheel of Fortune usually denotes unexpected sudden gain, happiness, success, or material prosperity. It has the connotation of something deserved or earned spiritually. On a deeper level, it can also mean the gaining of wisdom and balance. It is seldom ever unfortunate, unless very badly placed with the Devil or the Moon, then it can mean that great benefits are being delayed by your negative attitude to life.

11. Justice – *"As ye Sow Shall ye Reap"*

This is the "Karma" card which can also mean that the Enquirer will gain great prestige or renown. It also signifies that the Enquirer has a well-balanced outlook. It symbolizes, like the Hermit card, a trial of conscience, as well as meaning an actual trial, justice, and honesty. It also denotes the vindication of your moral integrity. When with the Hermit, it could denote a high legal position and if accompanied by the Emperor—a leader of government.

12. The Hanged Man –

Spiritual Sacrifice Brings Inner Peace

Not always a happy card, it means renunciation of both actual and spiritual self-sacrifice and abandonment. It can also mean that a difficult moral decision results in inner peace. It denotes occult power, intuition, and wisdom from above. On a more superficial level it can mean a suspended decision, pause, or calm.

13. Death – *The Transformation*

This card originally stood for the death of kings and princes and, although it can mean death, it carries a more positive meaning in today's world. It means more transformation, change, or positive destruction. It can herald a new life or mean the beginning of new creative activity.

14. Temperance – *Combination*

This card stands for adaptation to circumstances and the successful combination of new elements with old. It can mean simply a position of management. It is a happy card, bringing fruitfulness, new life, and vitality. It can also mean wealth and a successful marriage, or it can denote a balanced personality.

15. The Devil – *Irrevocable Event*

This card, although powerful, is not always unfortunate. It depends upon the integrity and spirituality of the Enquirer. If the Strength card is present, it can simply mean that a sudden, unexpected, and irrevocable event will alter future plans. However, it also stands for the domination of the material world over the spiritual. It can bring violence, catastrophe, illness, and almost overwhelming temptation, which will be difficult to resist. Not surprisingly, it also means the gratification of the lusts of the body at the expense of higher nature.

16. The Tower – *The Phoenix Rising*

This card always means suddenness. It can signify the end of selfish ambitions, sudden disruption, or a blow of fate; or show there is a karmic meaning at the end of life's lessons and a spiritual attainment that leads to a higher existence. On a more mundane level, it can simply mean abrupt and unexpected change, which could alter the pattern of life, or overthrow present plans. It always carries the connotation of something better once the dust has settled, even when surrounded by other negative cards.

17. The Star – *Rebirth of Joy, Love, and Hope*

This card is never negative. It means unselfish help given, hope, and optimism. This can manifest itself with renewed effort after disappointment, the courage to try again (particularly after a broken marriage), new inspiration for the artist, or renewed health for the invalid. It can mean, if placed with a negative card, that the Enquirer tends to give in to pessimism or intolerance through fear.

18. The Moon – *The Subconscious World of Dreams*

This card symbolizes illusion, deception, and things hidden below the surface. This can take the form of different things, such as mental illness and cancer. It also symbolizes the sea and the east. Although it is often a negative card, there is also the meaning of creativity and artistic imagination. When it is negative, it can mean a crisis of faith, which only the Enquirer can deal with, or misfortune or an accident happening to loved ones. It can be a warning that common sense should triumph over an hyperactive imagination.

19. The Sun – *Triumph and Success*

This card is always happy and, like the Chariot, means triumph after effort, but as a culmination. It means the end of study, freedom from restriction, and the realization of ambition. This can be coupled with fame and success. One of its most attractive meanings is the gift of gratitude for life's benefits. It is unalterable and modifies any surrounding negative cards.

20. The Judgment – *New Life / Rebirth*

This is always a good card. It means renewal or rebirth. It can also mean the intellectual and spiritual awakening that precedes happiness and fulfilment. It is a highly spiritual card meaning regrowth, progress, and getting out of a rut. Or, on a more mundane level, it can mean a beneficial change of work. If with Justice, or the Hermit and the Lovers, it can mean a divorce. But if it is with the Devil or the Moon, it could also mean the change or benefit may or may not be lasting, depending on the moral strength of the Enquirer.

21. The World – *Hearts Desire*

This is the card of the perfectionist. It is the "wish" card of the Major Arcana, bringing the Enquirer love, joy, happiness, and completion. It can also denote long journeys on water. If negatively placed, it means the Enquirer is unable to change his or her life patterns because of attachment to certain conditions and places. However, these will be overcome in time.

0. The Fool – *The Divine Questing Child*

This card means spiritual guidance through life or a vital choice that has to be made. It also denotes travel or movement, sometimes meaning a spiritual journey. If placed negatively, it can also mean extravagance, eccentricity, or a rebellion against the conventional authority. This card highlights the irresponsible element in human nature. Sometimes, although it denotes the Enquirer is highly spiritual, it can also mean that he or she is aimlessly wandering through life without a goal.

THE MYSTIC STAR SPREAD

As you are using a limited number of cards, some of the court cards adopt dual meanings: they will still represent people, but they will have subsidiary meanings:

Queen of Cups *stands for the wife or a happy marriage*
King of Cups *stands for the husband*
King of Swords *stands for a government official or a foreigner*
Knight of Staves *stands for emigration or a long journey*
Queen of Swords *stands for a widow or a foreign country*
Knight of Cups *stands for a proposal*
Knave of Swords *stands for being watched or being a deliberate thinker*
Queen of Coins *stands for the mother*

They also retain their previous meanings, so it will be necessary to work around them. To do this, you will have to:

- Use either the suit of Coins or Staves (which have fewer auxiliary meanings) for the Enquirer;
- Substitute the Knight of Coins for the Knight of Staves, but always remember that most of the court cards have other meanings.

The Reading

1. *Choose the appropriate card for the Enquirer, place it on the table and shuffle the pack. Hand it to the Enquirer and ask him or her to make three random cuts, then place the three piles face down on the table with the left hand.*
(The left hand is the hand of the Devil as it was once called, or—in modern psychological terms—the hand of the deep Unconscious, which motivates our conscious behavior.)

2. *Turn the three packs upward, and read the three cards individually and in combination.* These are thought to give a general indication of whether the reading will be fortunate or otherwise. (For the purpose of the reading illustrated here, we have chosen a female Enquirer—the Queen of Staves.)

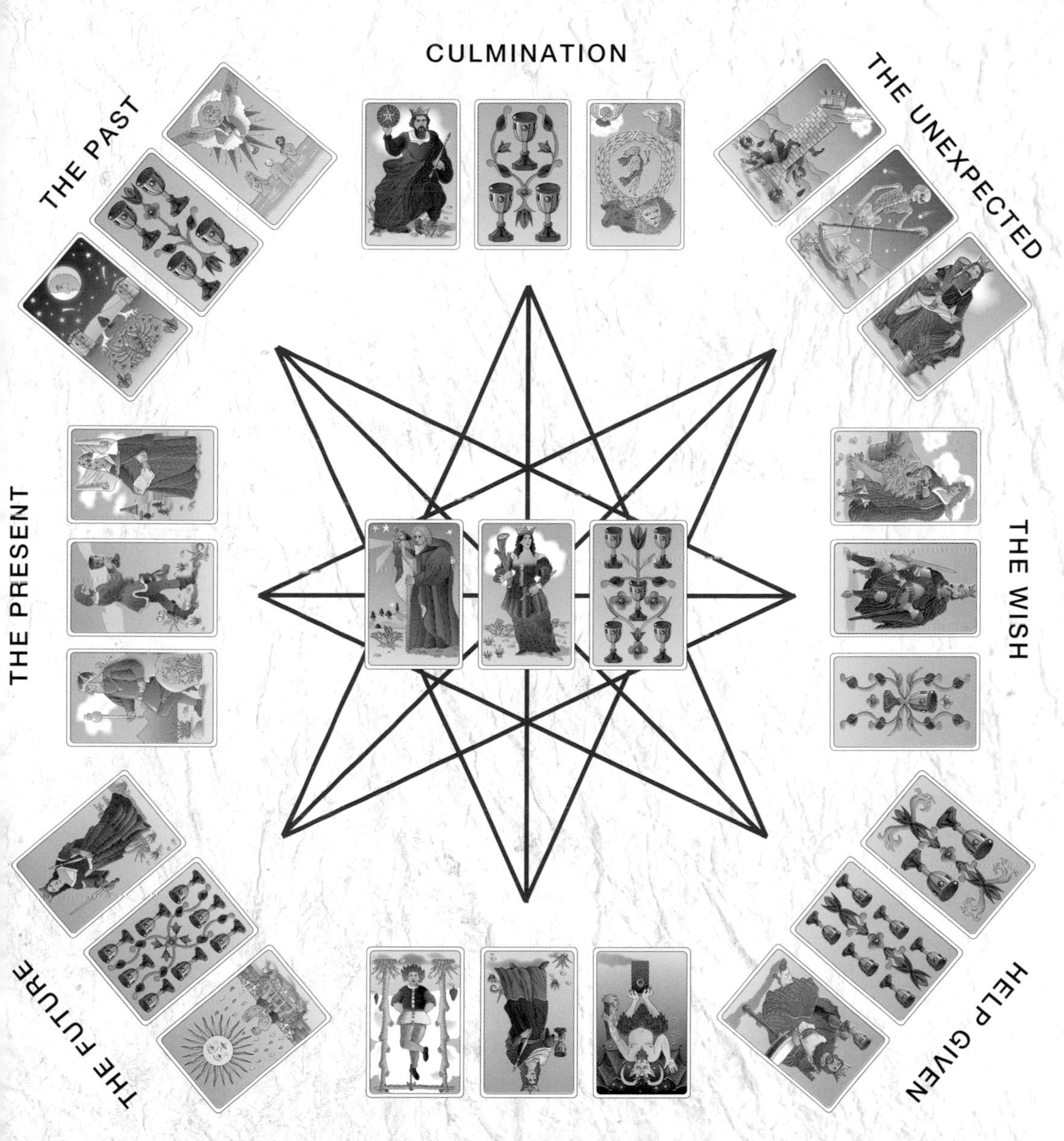
CULMINATION
THE PAST
THE UNEXPECTED
THE PRESENT
THE WISH
THE FUTURE
HELP GIVEN
THE HINDRANCES

3. *Lay out eight cards, keeping the Enquirer's card in the middle, in a counterclockwise direction, as in the illustration on page 75.*
Each point of the star deals with a different aspect of the reading.

4. *Now hand back the pack to the Enquirer and ask him or her to shuffle the pack again and then to lay two cards on top of the first eight cards.*
There will now be eight piles of three cards, and the Enquirer's card in the middle. Pick two cards yourself at random from the pack and cover the Enquirer's card, so that there will be twenty-seven cards laid out in the Spread.
You, the Reader, turn over the three cards in the first pile, starting with pile number two, "The Past," and read each pile, linking them together to make a story.
The two cards covering the Enquirer's card can be very important, as they can weaken or strengthen the Wish or the Culmination. They can also act as a check or a timely warning as to the wisdom of future actions of the Enquirer.

The Meaning

In the illustration given on page 75, the three cards in **Past**—the Moon, the Four Cups, and Judgment—could denote that the Enquirer has endured a separation or a divorce after deception and is not happy with the present situation.

In **Present**, there could be a new start at work, possibly in government. The Enquirer could be a teacher, or nurse, or even work with a big publisher in the future.

In **Future**, the Enquirer could be meeting a lover in a foreign country, perhaps while on holiday.

In **Hindrance**, it is possible to read these cards as meaning there will be some upheaval and sacrifice in business, which will interfere with the progress of the romance.

It could also be read that a sudden serious issue will come up over religion, which would entail sacrifice on either partner's part.

In **Help Given**, there will be an old friend or family member who will bring about reconciliation.

The **Wish** shows that strength will be needed, and that the Enquirer has that sufficient moral strength to overcome all obstacles. A happy marriage with a foreigner will be the result.

The **Unexpected** certainly is unexpected. It has the Tower among the three cards, as well as Death. It could mean simply that there will be a sudden death of a man, or it could mean that the life of the man in question will be transformed from being a bachelor to a model husband, and that the man could be a professional man or wearing a uniform.

Culmination is happy and all that the Enquirer would ask for. The rejoicing of the Three of Cups is accompanied by both the long journey card, and the King of Pentacles. So now we have a picture of the lover he or she will meet and know that they will accompany them overseas.

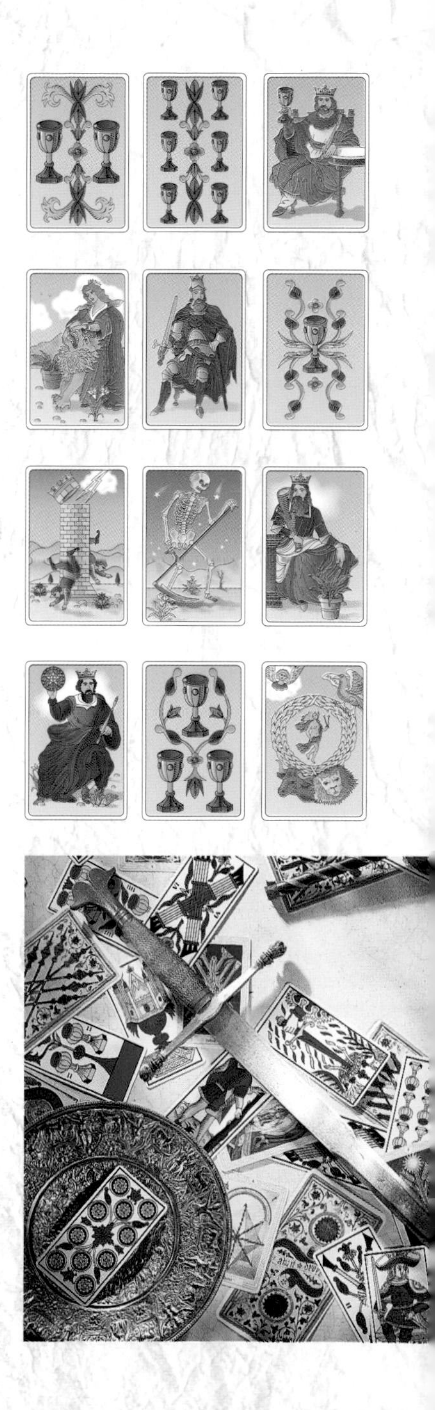

Now, the two cards that cover the Enquirer are the Hermit and the Five of Cups, which very clearly show indecision, perhaps the need for caution. But, more strongly, it gives the suggestion that the Enquirer tends to lack confidence in a decision and, instead of asking other people, the Enquirer must listen to his or her own intuition or lose the chance of happiness.

This gives a detailed example of what you might get in a spread. Use all the meanings of the cards given in this section to practice reading the cards. Regular practice is needed to be able to construct a coherent story from the cards, And, above all, good luck!

CHAPTER 4

love spells

Legions of the lovelorn down through the ages have bequeathed to us a variety of magic spells which were believed to bring back an errant lover, reveal the identity of a future marriage partner, or presage a future wedded state. Much of their appeal for us today must be the knowledge that we humans have always suffered and sought for love.

So, go on! The spells are fun and they have a fair rate of success. You never know, they might work for you—perhaps all you need to have is a positive belief in the power of magic!

SPELLS, RITUALS,

...and incantations

An Ozark mountain tradition reveals how to gain a person's love. On the night of the full moon you walk beneath your beloved's window. There you whisper his or her name three times to the night wind. From that moment on, this person will gaze at you through the eyes of love.

Spell casting is a magical procedure that manifests your intentions. Spells do work and they are not all difficult to pull off. All you need is some privacy, ten or fifteen minutes, a goal to accomplish, a few ordinary objects, and an extraordinary measure of concentration and determination.

Hallowe'en parties were popular in colonial America—apples were used from the plentiful supply collected at harvest to play games that divined future romances and marriages.

But just because you can make something happen, doesn't mean that you should do it. Who really wants a mate who is easy to trick, or a companion who runs off the moment the spell wears off? It is wrong to force affection from a person who doesn't care, who isn't ready to be involved, or who is attached to someone else. This type of magic is an inappropriate application of energy. Besides it's said that the magic you create comes back to you threefold.

So it's agreed that you don't have the right to change others, not their actions, their feelings, nor their minds. Ethically you are not to endanger others or yourself in any manner. But there's no harm in attracting someone who is already on the lookout for a loving partner, indeed it's advisable to create magical paths so that your soul mate can find you with ease.

Ultimately great lovers end up with great lovers. When you have great love to give, the universe sends an individual with the capacity to receive it. Throughout life your loving nature grows, and perhaps the person you've married is there to enhance your deepening love. Maybe you need more time to clarify your love nature, and your perfect partner will come along later.

The best way to become a great lover is to be true to your self. Within your own being you have everything necessary to please and be pleased by another person. These qualities magically appear as you eliminate those actions that demean and belittle others. It's easy to see that, as you reduce the shadows in yourself, the radiance of your love shines brighter for all.

APPLES

Apple peel

This is a method that is very simple and quick and may throw some light on who your future lover will be.

Peel an apple in one long strip.

Gently throw it over your shoulder onto the floor behind you.

If it assumes the shape of a letter, this will be the initial of your future lover's first name.

Apple seeds

This is another very simple, quick spell and could help you make a decision between two potential lovers.

Press an apple seed to your face and name a potential future partner.

Keep doing this for all your potential partners.

The one that sticks to your face the longest will be the one for you.

Apples on a string

This would be great fun to play with a large group of single friends.

Each person has to tie a piece of string to an apple and then twirl it in front of a fire.

The person whose string breaks first wins and is most likely to get married soon.

NUTS

Nuts can also be used in the pursuit of love, for example, the double-kernel hazelnut. Offer one kernel to the person who is the object of your affection and eat the other yourself. If you both remain silent until you've finished eating the nuts, you will be assured of a good friend or a future lover.

Is my lover faithful?

This is an old spell that told of whether love and trust is being misplaced.

Find two hazelnuts and name one for yourself and one for your lover.
Place the two hazelnuts side by side on a grate in a fireplace.
If the hazelnuts fail to burn, your lover does not love you.
If they fly apart, your lover has been unfaithful.
If they burn steadily at the same rate, you can expect a happy marriage to your lover.

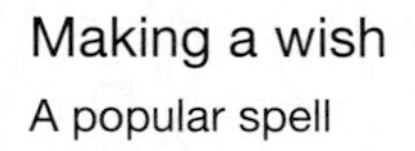

Making a wish

A popular spell

Find a nut and throw it onto a fire.
While doing so, make a wish in your head.
If the nut catches fire, then your wish will come true, as long as nobody else knows what you wished for.

OAKS AND MISTLETOE

In ancient times, the oak tree and mistletoe were considered magical and were held sacred by the Druids. Mistletoe was mysterious as it grew in places seemingly devoid of nourishment from the earth. Its leaves also grow in patterns of three, which was traditionally considered to be a perfect number.

Acorns as used in magical practices:

Find two acorns and fill a large bowl of water.

Drop the acorns into the bowl.

If they jump together, you and your lover will stay together.

If they jump apart, you and your lover will part ways

Mistletoe can mean peace, protection, and healing.

If you place a piece of mistletoe under your pillow on Midsummer's Eve, you will dream of your future partner.

Freya—goddess of love in Scandinavian mythology, wife of Odin. Friday is named for her.

Nature has always been considered to have magical properties. Flowers and leaves were and still are used in many spells, possibly because they are easily available.

FLOWERS

"My love is like a red, red rose."

Red roses have symbolized love ever since the ancient Greek goddess, Aphrodite, trod on white roses while hurrying to help her wounded lover, Adonis. A thorn pierced her foot and her blood turned the roses red. This was believed to be the origin of red roses and their connection with love.

Red rose

There is a rather difficult spell that involves a red rose. The rose is picked before seven o'clock in the evening of Midsummer's Eve and placed on a sheet of clean paper. If the rose is still fresh on Christmas Day—there's the difficulty—you should wear it to church. Then, you can rest assured, your future spouse will approach and claim the red rose.

Bachelor's button

This is a custom for the men. Place a small cutting of the plant, bachelor's button, in your pocket. If it withers quickly, it is an indication that your choice of maiden is unwise. Girls—you can hide bachelor's button about your person to attract love.

Blossom

A rather more manageable spell is to pick a blossom in June, place it in an envelope and seal with wax. The wax has to be sealed with your ring finger (the third finger of the left hand). The envelope should then be placed under your pillow. Any dreams should be carefully noted down, but don't worry if you don't have any dreams the first night—the envelope can stay under your pillow for seven nights. The dreams you have during this time could signify the following:

Water, fields, flowers, mountains, glass, children, parents, organ music, or the moon mean you will get married within the year.

Animals, fish, birds, giants, paper, mirrors, or the sun mean you will have to wait five years to get married.

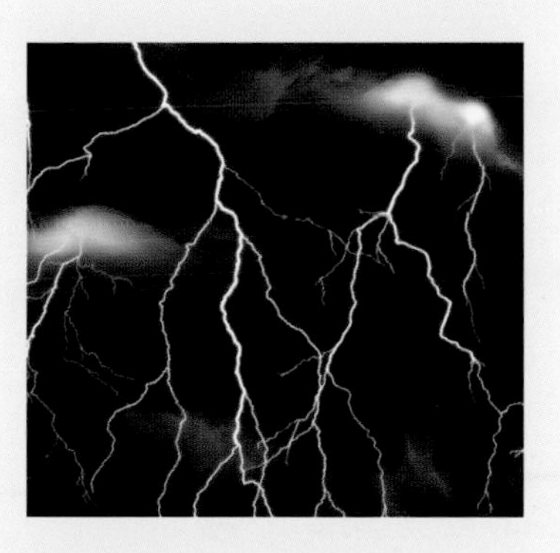

Bells, gold, storms, reptiles, or soldiers mean you won't get married in the foreseeable future.

HERBAL SPELLS

As well as being used in the culinary arts and in the sick room, herbs have also always been thought to possess magical qualities and can be used in many spells.

Rosemary

Traditionally it was said that rosemary, sage, and parsley only grew where the mistress was master. A sprig of rosemary used to be woven into a bridal bouquet to ensure fidelity. Sometimes rosemary was dipped into the newlywed's wine at the wedding feast to ensure lifelong happiness.

Place a sprig of rosemary and a real silver coin under your pillow before going to sleep. You will then dream of your future lover.

Sage

Sage is another herb used in foretelling the future and is considered extremely potent by those who practice magic. It is believed that if, at exactly midnight on Christmas Eve, a girl goes into the garden and plucks twelve sage leaves, one for every stroke of the hour, making sure the leaves are undamaged, she will then be rewarded with a shadowy apparition of her future husband.

The Wedding Day, a lithograph from circa 1885

PLANTS

Myrtle

Myrtle has always been associated with love, marriage, and fertility, as it is one of two plants under the protection of Venus. The other plant is the rose. Myrtle is placed in wedding bouquets to ensure fertility. Bridesmaids might take some of the myrtle from the wedding bouquet and plant it in their garden. If the cutting grows, the next wedding they go to will be their own.

Laurel

A charming custom is for a loving couple to pick a twig of laurel and break it in two. They each keep a piece and it is supposed to keep their love alive.

Yarrow

This is an old tradition that unmarried girls used to carry out on the eve of May Day. Pick nine sprigs of yarrow early in the morning and say,

Good morrow, fair Yarrow,
And thrice good morning to thee,
Come tell me before tomorrow,
Who my true love shall be.

Then take the yarrow home, put it in your right stocking and place it under your pillow. It is believed you will, that night, dream of your future husband. However, if you utter a single word after picking the yarrow, the spell will not work.

Holly

The female holly plant can be used in a similar way to foretell the future. Gather leaves in silence late on a Friday and bring them home in a three-cornered scarf or handkerchief. When inside your house, choose nine of the leaves and place them carefully under the pillow of the one seeking love. Any dreams that night are considered prophetic.

Hawthorn and St. John's Wort

Hawthorn has been traditionally connected with May Day and was also considered to offer protection against witchcraft.

On May Day in Norfolk, young girls would gather bunches of hawthorn blossom for luck in love, but they had to carry them home in silence, or they would not marry that year. However, St. John's Wort, gathered on Saint John's Eve, could change that, provided the pretty, yellow flowers were picked while the dew was still on them.

When you question the intentions of a lover, you could recite the traditional saying: "He or she loves me, or loves me not" as you remove the petals of a daisy. It is doubtful that you base any decision upon the outcome of this superstitious act. More often, consulting the daisy oracle just calms your mind, as you wait for a response.

SUPERSTITIONS AND OMENS

Learning to respect ancient superstitions and interpret the omens

Looking closer at our beliefs about divination, we find that they fall into two basic attitudes. The first view is dependency. We are not sure that omens tell us the truth, but we consult them because the ritual is comforting. The second outlook is fear. We sense the truth of these messages, but we fear the means by which the answers come to us. Neither of these attitudes deal effectively with the unknown. Neither reflects the true nature of magic.

Our universe is inherently magical. Nature is constantly communicating with us through its forces and changing appearances. And technology has its unique ways of attracting our attention. It's up to us to notice the subtle signs around us. It's our responsibility to interpret them in a way that benefits us and those we love. If we only view these signs externally, we will never thoroughly understand them. If we ask for inner guidance, the spiritual aspect of life is seen.

The human race has generated millions of superstitions. Most are attempts to handle magic and the unknown. Some of these strange ideas are based on emotions like fear and hatred. Those beliefs try to restrain us from gaining a wider experience of life. Other beliefs rest firmly on physical realities or higher spiritual principles, but their wisdom has not yet been revealed.

As a lover you make your own luck through living by your intentions. Your harvests cannot be expected to be any different from the seeds you plant. If your relationships support negative and separatist beliefs, the outcome will be a disturbed life. If your heart is opened wide to the possibilities of spiritual growth and greater awareness, the vistas are unimaginable. Choose your omens well and reap the benefits.

LUCKY ANIMALS

Squirrel *To see a squirrel means happiness is near.*

Lamb *To meet a solitary lamb symbolizes love, peace, and prosperity.*

Cock crowing *To hear a cock crowing while thinking of your lover is a good sign.*

Dove *A sign of bliss and contentment in love*

Mouse *To be presented with a white mouse by one who is unaware of the significance of the gift will bring happiness in love.*

Sparrow *A fortunate bird for lovers*

Many superstitions are not taken too seriously today, but don't let this stop you from trying out these cheeky little numbers...

HOLLY LEAVES

- Take three leaves of holly; prick the initials of your admirers on them with a pin; place them under your pillow; and go to sleep. The admirer you dream about will be your future spouse.

- Tie a sprig of holly to each leg of your bed and, before you go to bed, eat a baked apple. Your future husband will be revealed to you in your dreams.

NOTABLE DAYS FOR LOVERS

In the past, there were special days for superstitions. Events like New Year's Eve had their own rituals. Many of them involved ways of seeing your future husband or wife or predicting an early wedding. For example, it was once believed that a girl drinking the last glass from a bottle as the clock struck midnight on New Year's Eve would be the next bride in the house. Here are some more:

St. Valentine's Day

If you meet someone of the opposite sex on this day, you will find a true lover within three months and, if he or she is unmarried, it could be your future spouse. If you have no valentines, take two bay leaves sprinkled with rosewater and lay them on your pillow when you go to bed. Put on clean nightclothes, making sure that they are inside out, then say "In dreams good valentine be kind to me and let me this one night my true love see."

New Year's Day

Should you get out of bed and, looking out your window, see a person of the opposite sex, you will be married within the year.

May Day

"The girl who on the first of May,
goes to the fields at break of day,
and washes in dew from the hawthorn tree,
ever more beautiful shall she be."

At dawn on May 1 search for a garden snail, and place it by the ashes of a dead fire. If the snail draws in its horns and refuses to move, there will be no romance for you. If it crawls away, it will leave a trail in the shape of an initial that will indicate your future love.

The night of October 31 is the eve of All Saints' Day, known as Hallowe'en. It is a great opportunity for a party—dressing up and wearing a mask. But for lovers it is a more significant time, for on this night you might find out who will be your future spouse, or become aware of symbols of your future life.

HALLOWE'EN

The magical date of October 31st

Hallowe'en Lucky Dip

Mashed potato is the traditional dish. Place six charms in it. Then turn out all lights and each guest, armed with a spoon and fork, must try to find the following hidden charms:

a ring – *marriage*
a coin – *wealth*
a button – *bachelorhood*
a heart-shaped charm – *passionate love*
a shell – *long journeys*
a key – *great success and power*

To see your future partner at Hallowe'en

When you go to bed, take a lighted candle into a darkened room. Sit in front of a mirror either eating an apple or combing your hair. After a few minutes, it is said that you will see in the mirror image the face of your future partner looking over your shoulder.

Bobbing for apples

Each person is given an apple from which a small piece has been cut to allow a fortune, written on a small slip of paper, to be placed inside. The apples are thrown into a large tub of water and you are invited to dunk your head and grab an apple with your mouth. There's one catch—your arms must be behind your back! Then read aloud your fortune, which, of necessity, is brief, such as "Beware of the tall man who professes to be your friend," or "You will marry a woman of great learning."

TALISMANS

Averting danger and bringing good fortune

Hand of Fatima—believed to bring luck and avert evil

In this treatise on magic for lovers, only one question remains. Can magic be used to protect love? Love itself needs no protection, but relationships are another matter.

Each love relationship has a specific purpose and runs by its own clock. The secret of being a great lover is to sense and work with the energy within a particular relationship. This means sharing what you have with your mate, and gratefully receiving what your partner gives you. It also means accepting your relationship as it is today and evolving with it.

When you find that special someone, you try to make the most of your time together. You want these occasions to be positive and constructive. The state of any love relationship reflects the intentions of the partners involved. It will never be any more or any less. No two people enter a relationship for the same reasons. It's up to each couple to determine and act on their shared values. If the intentions of lovers cannot mesh in a concerted manner, the relationship will not endure.

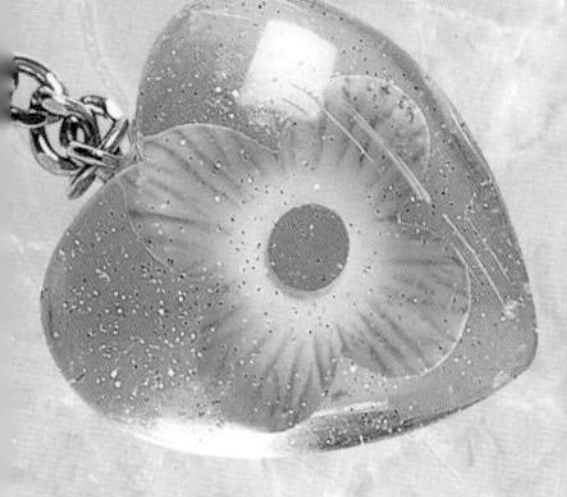

Heart *Considered to be the seat of the soul and the symbol of universal love. It is worn to bring joy.*

Fish *An ancient Egyptian charm to promote domestic bliss.*

Eye beads *Shaped like an eye in blue glass and onyx and thought to promote love affairs*

Amber beads *Thought to be lucky for brides*

Frog *This talisman from ancient Rome is worn to promote mutual ardour and ensure happy relationships*

Magic is the art of making your intentions real. One astounding way you can honor your shared intentions is through the creation of love talismans. This ancient magical art deliberately charges an object with the love energy that is shared. The item could be something natural that you've found together, or it may be a symbolic object that the two of you create. Through your joined efforts, you embody your intentions into this object representing your love.

Talismans help us connect with natural and powerful forces. If you dare, you can invoke the protection of angels, divas, and deities, but be prepared for the unimaginable. What if your lover is not the least bit interested in using magic? In that case simply state your own intentions to be the best lover and partner possible. You may ask for your union be blessed, guided, and protected in all ways. And from that, your lover gains as well.

THE PENTACLE

The five-pointed star or pentacle, which is a form of the Seal of Solomon, has long been believed to have great occult powers. It is symbolized as a guide to great achievement and also a protection of bodily health.

THE TALISMAN OF VENUS

A very powerful talisman in ancient Greece was what is now known as The Talisman of Venus (the goddess of love was known to the ancient Greeks as Aphrodite, only later was she sometimes known by her Roman name of Venus). Venus was the goddess of beauty, fertility, and sexual love. If you want the talisman to bring you luck in love, draw the seal of the Goddess Venus on parchment or thick paper and carry it around with you, particularly when traveling.

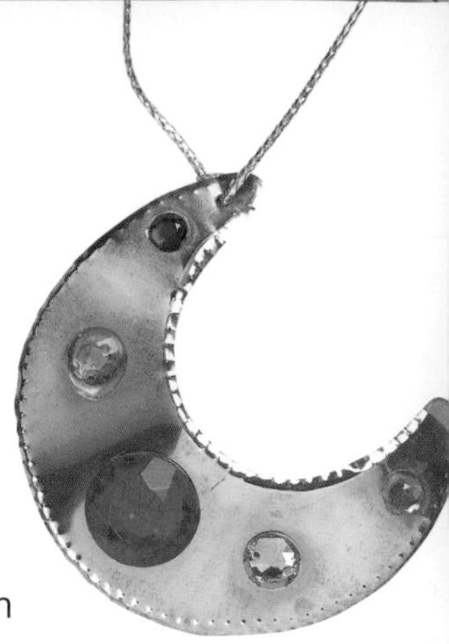

Jewels have always been highly valued not only for their beauty, but also for their rarity and ancient symbolism. Since the earliest civilizations, people have believed that precious stones possess magical and astrological significance. Many amulets and talismans containing gems were made to protect the wearer from the evil eye and to bring protection and relief from illness, while others were worn to attract love and to bring good fortune to the lover.

MAGIC PROPERTIES OF STONES

The power and meaning of beautiful stones

PRECIOUS AND SEMIPRECIOUS STONES

Today's lovers are often influenced by the meanings behind gemstones. Look, for example, at the significance of a ring or a solitaire diamond.

Aquamarine Its name comes from words meaning seawater, or blue-green, because to the Romans its color resembled the sea. They believed this semiprecious stone to be a lucky keystone for seafarers and a jewel that brought harmony into marriage.

Diamond Diamonds are the queen of jewels, cut to enhance the internal reflection and refraction of light to produce a sparkling brilliance. Roman warriors often wore diamonds bound to their left arm to give them courage in battle, but it was also believed to be the lover's stone and was worn to promote constancy and fortitude through the trials of married life and to promote reconciliation.

Emerald It was believed that outright treachery would cause this beautiful green precious stone to crumble in its setting, and that a lover's deception or inconstancy would dim its luster. It was also believed to ward off dangers and lessen the pain of childbirth.

Sapphire This precious stone, mentioned in the Bible, is a beautiful variety of corundum. It was thought to promote mental health and to strengthen the heart if worn over it. It was also said to guard the wearer's chastity and, at the approach of treachery or evil, would dim in warning.

Garnet This dark red, semiprecious stone is the emblem of constancy and faithfulness between lovers and friends.

Turquoise Mainly from Persia (modern-day Iran), this semiprecious stone is considered to be the luckiest one for lovers, as it was supposed to promote peace and harmony in marriage, as well as giving protection against the evil intentions of others. In the past, Persian horsemen used to wear it to ensure both surefootedness and safety.

Sardonyx Like the emerald, the semiprecious sardonyx was thought to lessen the pain of childbirth. In ancient Rome, brides wore this stone to bring marital happiness.

Jet A compact form of coal, jet was believed to have curative properties for the female. It was worn as a protection against hysteria and female disorders, and as a counter-agent to magical spells and occult influences.

CHAPTER 5

more magic & dreams

There are many ways of foretelling the future and reading the signs of love. Not all of them can be discussed in this book; however, this final chapter gives an overview of symbols, omens, and codes—you can use it constructively to prepare yourself for happiness and protect yourself from possible disappointments. Heed the advice of this soothsayer and greater strength and self-understanding will be your reward.

Should you share your dreams with your lover? Only the most accepting couple can handle hearing each other's dreams without misunderstandings. For instance, the people in our dreams do not refer to the actual people in our life; they are our feelings about them. These situations are not to be taken at face value. Having a dream about an individual is often a way to heal old wounds. So dreaming about our ex-husband or ex-wife doesn't mean we want to remarry this flame of ages past.

LOVERS IN DREAMLAND

The meaning of dreams

In case you were wondering, there are three types of dream. The first kind of dream is simply our restless mind going over the unsettled matters of the day. It is usually jumbled and strange. The second kind of dream is the dramatization. It attempts to work out our unsolved problems, especially with the types of people you don't understand or accept. The third sort of dream is a message of inner guidance. It reveals the next step in our spiritual development. The last type of dream involves the collective destiny of humanity. It affects us profoundly.

No one can really interpret our dreams for us, not even our lovers. We can be assisted in recalling details or noticing patterns, but we are the final authority on our dreams. Some symbols listed in dream dictionaries may be specific to a particular culture, and if we don't share those beliefs, the symbolism won't relate to us. Some of our dream content refers to those universal symbols common to all humans; other images like memories are peculiar to our own experience.

How do we understand our dreams? We start by recording them the moment we wake. Then over time we track the various symbols and observe how they are used. At a certain point something rather magical happens. As we become intimately familiar with the elements used by our unconscious, a language takes shape and a two-way communication develops. Each night as we go to sleep we ask for guidance. Each morning we awake inspired with a new dream message.

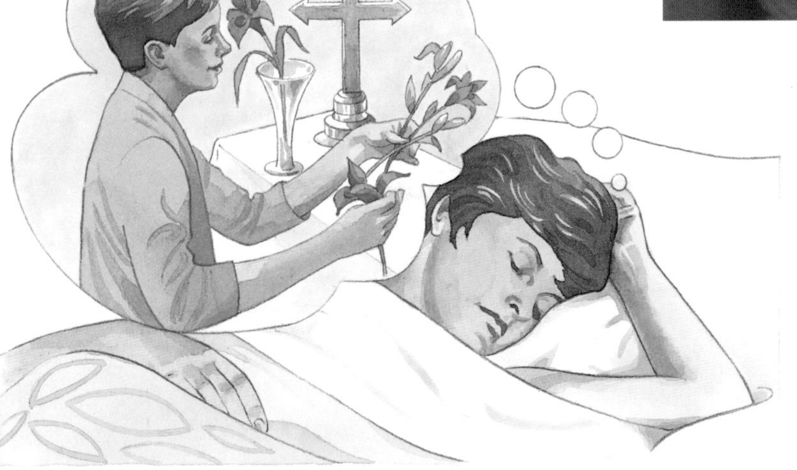

Altar *An unhappy dream if you are standing before it—signifying loss and illness. However, if you are decorating an altar, a happy love affair is in the offing.*

INTERPRETING COMMON SYMBOLS IN DREAMS

People and Animals

Adder To be bitten by a snake or adder implies treachery from a false friend. To see yourself killing an adder means an end to an undesirable friendship.

Cat Deceit from a loved one or a lucky meeting at night, depending on the sensation either of revulsion or affection you feel for the animal in your dream.

Birth The end of one chapter or love affair, and the start of another.

Oyster A luxurious and wealthy marriage.

Horse White horses running means a wonderful lover awaits you. However, if you fall from the horse or cannot mount it, then your affair will be passionate but short-lived.

Bachelor To talk to a bachelor means there will be a wedding soon; but a married man dreaming he is again a bachelor warns of his future unfaithfulness.

Quail Many selfish love affairs causing great unhappiness.

Baby For a woman to dream of a baby means great joy and true love is coming. If a man dreams he is nursing a baby, a bitter disappointment in love awaits him.

Frog A lucky dream for the lover—meaning a happy marriage.

Cocks If a cock crows, you have a false friend who is plotting to do you harm. If he is silent, beware—for you have a rival in love who is more powerful than he seems.

Deer If the deer runs away, you will deeply offend a loved one. If the deer comes toward you, there will be a reconciliation with a former lover.

Magpie This portends of a hasty and unhappy union. To dream of two or more magpies is unlucky, for it means there will be a death around the house. One magpie means a sudden betrothal; two magpies for a woman mean a wealthy husband.

Bull A warning—if you are too impetuous you will lose the person you have set your heart on.

Swallows A past lover returns—it is up to you whether he or she stays or flies away again.

Guests A crowd of unwanted guests means you will have unexpected good luck. To dream of guests is a happy augury, and if you yourself are the guest, you will travel to faraway places and great changes will take place in your life.

Blind man If you are leading the blind person, your trust is being betrayed by one you love. If you yourself are blind, your choice of a future mate will be unfortunate.

Fortune Teller To dream of a fortune teller, particularly of looking into a crystal, means that there are hidden things or hidden enemies in your life, which will be revealed to you in the nick of time.

Beard If a woman dreams she has grown a beard, she will soon be free of the attentions of an undesirable suitor.

Tiger A warning. Someone is coming into your life who will try to harm you.

Cuckoo If you hear but do not see the bird, someone will deliberately try to advise you wrongly. If you see the bird but it is silent, this means the arrival of a new love. But if it is singing, there will be quarrels and troubles with the old love before you meet the new.

Shaving To dream someone is shaving you denotes an unfaithful lover.

Moths To dream of moths is a warning that you are being led astray by happy-go-lucky company and both your reputation and your health will suffer.

Raven There are many disappointments ahead: this symbol means you will lose money and have a rival for your affections. It is an unlucky dream implying that you are surrounded by flatterers and deceit.

Eyes Sore and infected eyes mean the illness of a lover or close friend. Blindness denotes the loss of these.

Pigeon When flying, good news can be expected from a long distance. When roosting expect domestic harmony with a faithful partner.

Turtle Great mutual happiness and love.

Uniform A journey full of adventure will occur and will have a special romantic interest.

Bathing If the water is clear, your love affair will end happily. If it is dirty or muddy, there will be unexpected troubles surrounding your love life.

Barefoot To dream you are a beggar or are dressed in rags with bare feet means that considerable sacrifices will be asked of you in marriage, but the result will be well worthwhile.

Mouse Busybodies will try to interfere with your romantic affairs.

Butterfly Warning—your lover is fickle.

Nursery Wealth and prosperity through honest labor. To the married—a direct prophecy meaning a birth; to those in love—an early engagement and wedding.

Love To the lonely and single—an affair of the heart, possibly marriage. But to the engaged and married this dream is unlucky, signifying quarrels. To see others in love means you will quarrel with or become indifferent to these people.

Drinking To dream you are drunk denotes outstanding success. To dream of drinking alcohol denotes business losses, but the gain of a staunch ally. However, to dream you are drinking water means a bitter disappointment to your marital partner or lover.

Eagle Flying high means hopes come true, but if the bird is resting or comes to earth the lover will meet with disillusionment.

Dove To see a dove fall means the death of a former love or relative, but to see it flying is a dream of positive happiness, peace, and prosperity.

Kissing To kiss someone against their will means your lover is true, but if you yourself resent being kissed you will live without love.

Fingernails To dream of having them cut, or of short nails, is a dream signifying dishonor, disgrace and estrangement from friends, but if your nails are unusually long this denotes success in business and love affairs.

Dentist To dream of having a tooth pulled means a money loss. To dream of having a tooth filled means someone will lend you money. But to dream of false teeth or a hollow tooth means a worrying situation will be brought into the open.

House and Home

Window If you dream of watching from a window it signifies a reconciliation. If you see someone watching you through a window, slander will be directed toward you.

Path To dream of a broad, smooth path means extravagance, conceit, and unhappy love affairs. If you dream of a narrow, rough, and crooked path, it denotes success in life and love.

Clothes If you are well dressed, you will suffer the loss of money. If clothed in black—a great joy awaits you. If in white—much sorrow. However, if you see yourself in rags—your success is assured.

Knocking If you dream you are knocking or hammering on a door to gain entrance, you are committed to a hopeless cause and will only waste your life.

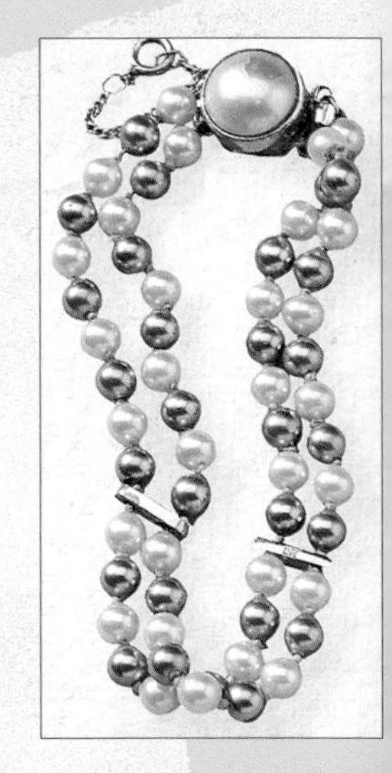

Attic This means a renewal of an old and trusted friendship. It also means you will move away from where you live to a busy place where, if you are not married, you will meet your future partner.

Jewelry If the dreamer has passed through a great grief, this is a happy dream meaning consolation from the love and devotion of another. For the lover this is not favorable—it means vanity will spoil many a romance.

Scissors To a married person, scissors mean a misunderstanding with their spouse. To a single person, it means an approaching wedding.

Ring If a wife dreams she has broken a jeweled ring, she will have a bitter quarrel with her husband.

Key A single key denotes love and marriage; a bunch means wealth but very little love.

House A new or strange dwelling means a contented spouse and domestic peace. To watch a house be demolished or fall signifies family discord and estrangements.

Broom To sweep with a broom denotes a great change in the life and occupation of the dreamer. To see a broom lying on the ground means the desertion of an old friend.

Clock If you see a clock, a cherished dream is coming nearer. If you hear one strike, a marriage proposal is imminent.

Bells Tolling bells bring bad news of a friend or distant relative. A bell that is silent signifies a sudden quarrel between married people.

Rope To dream you are bound by a rope means you will break a promise to a friend. To see others bound—you will be let down yourself.

Bed To dream you are in your own bed means that you have a period of hectic activity ahead of you that will advance your interests. To dream you are in a strange bed means that you will have to travel to attain your object or ambition, but there will be a stressful period before you set off.

Balcony To watch others on a balcony symbolizes future success in love. To see the balcony give way or to be standing on it when it does, means a bitter quarrel with your lover.

Safe An empty safe means an early marriage; a full safe means a late marriage. If you dream you are breaking open a safe, you will not marry the person with whom you are now in love.

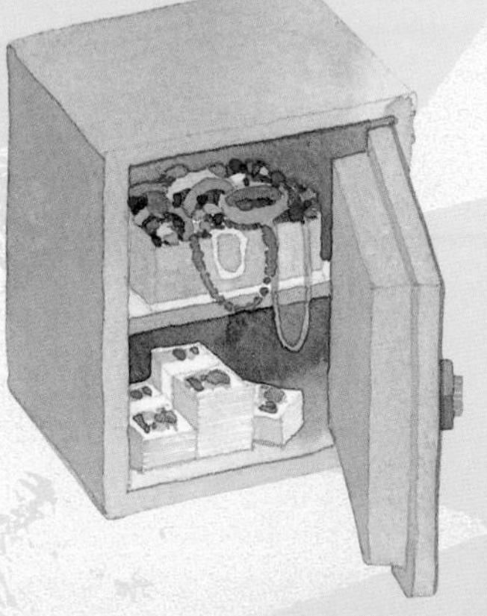

Cage If a woman dreams the cage is full of birds, she will receive a proposal of marriage. If it is empty, it symbolizes family opposition and an elopement or secret marriage. If the dreamer is a man, it foretells an early marriage.

Entertainment

Merry-go-round Life will become easier and more organized in the future if you dream of riding on a merry-go-round. However, if you dream you are in a deserted fairground and the merry-go-round is empty but still revolving, then your troubles are mainly your own fault and unless you do some serious thinking your energies will be frittered uselessly away.

Arrow If the dreamer is wounded—a confidence will be betrayed. If the dreamer is themselves shooting arrows—they must beware of telling lies in the future.

Trumpet To see a trumpet but not hear it means a great disappointment. But to hear it means your lover or friend is insincere in his affections.

Ball If you are playing ball, it means exceptionally good news, but to watch others playing suggests you will be jealous of a friend.

Cards If you are playing and know you will win, you will get married after a whirlwind love affair. If you lose, there will be danger ahead. If you are a spectator someone will attempt to defraud you.

Jigsaw To dream of doing a jigsaw means you will overcome great restrictions that have been impeding either your career or your progress with a lover.

Entertainment Even when not allied to the former dream, this means broken contracts in love and commerce.

Dancing To dream you are dancing means you will receive an unexpected present from a stranger. To dance alone denotes a single life; and to watch others dancing denotes jealousy in love.

Singing Unlucky for the lover. Sudden disturbing news can be expected.

The Natural World

Moon A new moon means unexpected happiness in love. A full moon suggests an approaching marriage.

Ice To those in love, this is an ominous dream meaning the end of a relationship.

Stars This is a lucky dream, if the stars are bright, that symbolizes great success in love and business. If the stars are dim or fading, the reverse applies.

Horns If you have grown horns, you will not marry for love.

Horseshoe Gambling losses and unrequited love.

Snow To an unmarried young girl, this dream means she will shortly meet the man she will marry.

Signs of the Zodiac Travel followed by marriage—you will settle in a foreign country.

Ocean If the ocean is rough it denotes turbulence in the household. If it is smooth you will reconcile two lovers who have been parted, and if the moon is shining, you will find love yourself.

Garden Marriage to a beautiful person.

Rainbow A bright rainbow foretells a brilliant marriage to someone who is famous and widely popular.

Flowers

Anemone You have a faithful lover.

Arum Lily Unhappiness in marriage.

Carnation A passionate affair is imminent.

Clover Someone who has little money but a good heart will want to marry you.

Crocus A dark man will prove a deceiver.

Daffodil You have been unfair and unjust to a lover—seek a reconciliation.

Honeysuckle Domestic quarrels.

Iris A letter will come with good news from your lover.

Rose Within a year a wedding—possibly your own.

Snowdrop Confide your secret to someone you trust.

Poppy Arrival of a message which will cause you great disappointment.

Fruit

Apricot Early marriage for the single—affectionate children for the married.

Cherry Unhappy circumstances in romantic affairs

Gooseberry Be warned—you have a rival.

Lemon Marital quarrels, separation, and broken engagements.

Orange A very unlucky dream signifying the loss of a lover through his or her infidelity.

Peach A lucky dream: love is reciprocated and you will enjoy good health.

Pear A new romantic friendship.

Raspberry Consolation from an unexpected source after a great disappointment.

Nut To dream you are eating nuts means you will bring your marriage partner to ruin through your own extravagance. If you see nuts growing, your marriage partner will grow richer through the years.

LOVE IN A TEACUP

The language of the leaves

There was a time when circles of acquaintances gathered in the parlor each afternoon for tea. When everyone had their fill of tea and gossip, those who dared peered into their empty teacups. The insights gained by this practice were often regarded as entertainment, but not always.

Tassiomancy or tea-leaf reading is a modern type of divination that discerns the future by giving meaning to seemingly random shapes. It is one of the simplest ways of foretelling the future and does not need any special skill or psychic knowledge. So how does it work?

There is an elaborate ritual connected with tea-leaf reading which was probably devised to impress the sitter with the solemnity and significance of the ceremony. It is not at all necessary to turn the cup around three times and then upend it, but it is more fun. All you need is a wide-mouthed cup, white on the inside, and a good brand of tea that does not deteriorate into dust. China tea is traditionally the best to use for this purpose.

As the heart shape is near the handle or "house," it could portend a thunderbolt of love.

A heart next to a fruit indicates some lighthearted enjoyment and an initial indicates a new lover.

The practice of reading is really quite simple. The leaves can form alphabet letters representing people's names. Or a pattern showing common objects may suggest upcoming events. Of course, the best omen for lovers is the heart...

All symbols must be taken together: a single symbol is rarely read alone; the presence of hearts, crosses, money dots, or other attendant symbols contribute to the final interpretation. For instance, while large dark clumps of tea leaves are never good omens, don't panic—there could be other tea-leaf pictures present which act to lessen their effect.

You will definitely see pictures if you concentrate. Your skills of interpretation may take time, but with practice you will soon begin to interpret the symbols accurately. You will come to realize that an important extra sense—your sixth sense—is lying dormant, waiting for you to bring it out and polish it up.

So, bring along an open mind, imagination, and the ability to interpret the facts and you will see the message in the tea leaves as easily as you see faces in the clouds. Try to let your head rule your heart, if only for as long as it takes to do a reading!

Heart at the end of a line of dots (roadway) indicates romance at the end of a long journey.

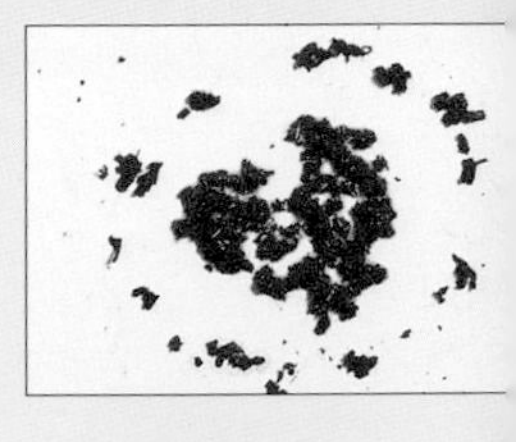

Heart surrounded by dots indicates the romance will be stormy.

Heart and dollar signs show romance and money.

Heart and ship indicate the object of romance is connected with sea or will meet their fate on a ship.

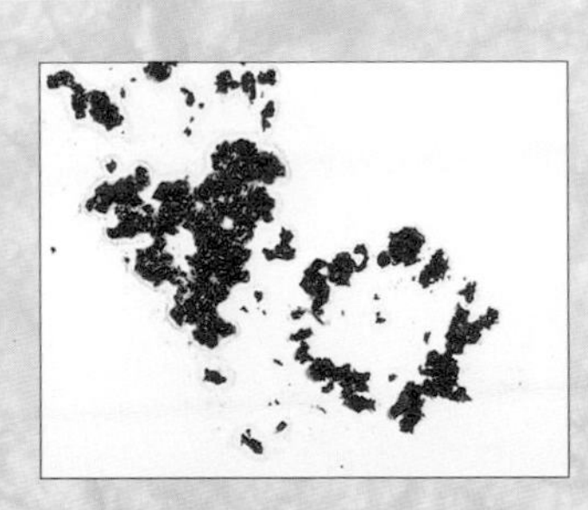

Two hearts together, one with a ring next to it or with lovebirds indicate a wedding.

The most important step is to relax. You can do this by closing your eyes and clearing your mind. All pressing concerns must be released and that includes questions about your love life. When you open your eyes to view the tea leaves, you want to be able to see the truth. With practice the various symbols will become clearer to your inner eye.

LUCKY TEA LEAVES

Auspicious signs do not just need to be present—they must be recognized as well.

Look hard for symbols of good omen! These are the lucky ones, and the ones that assure you of success in romance and financial affairs.

Rest assured that if you see one or more of these symbols in the tea cup then you will meet romance in the very near future.

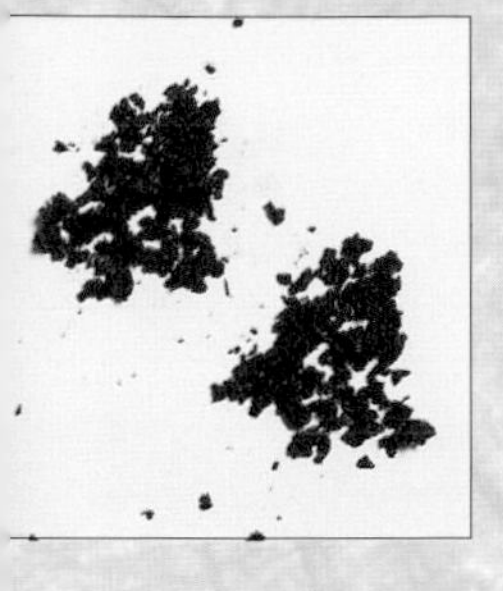

Bells *Two bells together mean a wedding bringing happiness and wealth.*

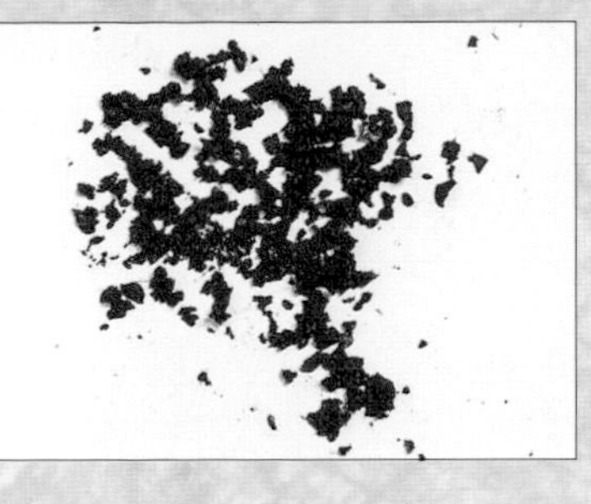

Bouquet *This means staunch friends, and a happy and wealthy marriage.*

An angel tells of fortunate, life-changing news from a loved one.

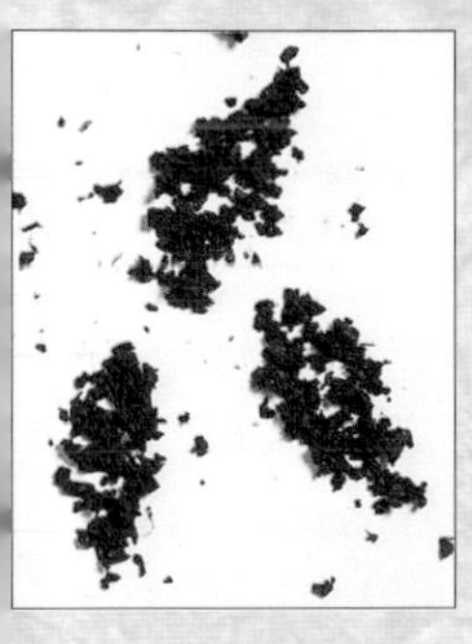

Leaves *A happy second marriage.*

Horseshoe *A lucky emblem concerned with romance when seen near the "house."*

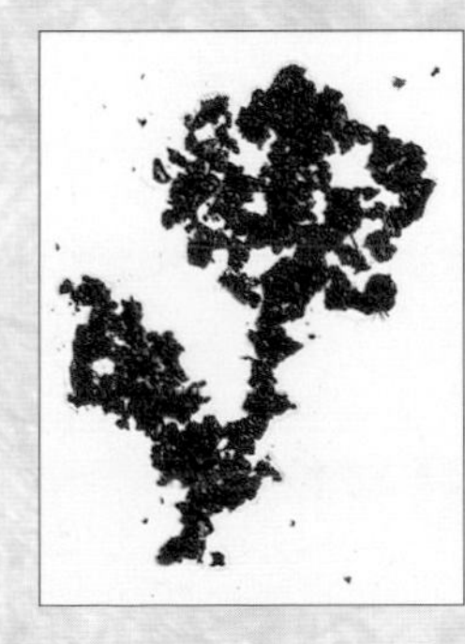

Rose *The fulfillment of the lover's hopes and wishes is assured.*

Lovers' knot or ribbon bow *means a new love interest and with a heart it means marriage.*

A lover's feelings can and do change. Negative symbols in the tea leaves act as a warning and could crystallize an intuition that a lover's passion has cooled.

WARNING TEA LEAVES

Advice to heed to avert disappointment in love

Some of these shapes may have more than one meaning depending upon their placement, so do not immediately assume that the association must be negative. For instance, a gun, although unfortunate in some circumstances, can simply indicate sudden news.

Keep in mind that these symbols of bad omen can be mitigated by other more fortunate symbols. Most are only a warning, allowing you to change an outcome by direct action, or lessen its impact by being prepared.

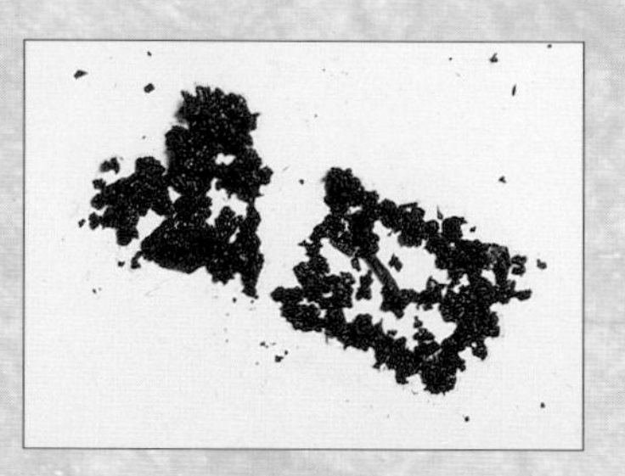

Letter *News from a lover, particularly when near a heart or close to an initial.*

Seesaw *Do not be disheartened. There will be many ups and downs in a love affair before it reaches its happy conclusion.*

Violet *Near a heart it means an unassuming, modest but true lover is coming into your life.*

Ball *The lover must try to stop taking the line of least resistance.*

Mouse *Someone who loves you is waiting for you. Show more courage in your pursuit.*

Owl *If near the "house" and at the top of the cup, a loved one's unfaithful conduct brings misery and sadness.*

Volcano *A warning against a lack of self-discipline and the need for discretion, because uncontrolled passion brings trouble in its wake.*

A fan is the symbol of flirtation. An open fan means deception on a grand scale from your beloved. If the fan is shut, there will be temporary deceit.

Wreck *If near the house or a heart or a ring, it means separation from a loved one.*

Yoke *This is the symbol of slavery. It warns that you are losing your own personality and interests by allowing someone else to dominate you.*

Weather vane *The symbol of inconstancy—if near a heart, it means a fickle lover.*

Mermaid *This spells danger to the lover, for an overwhelming attraction and temptation is about to arrive that could lead to his or her destruction.*

THE LANGUAGE OF FLOWERS

Lovers communicating without words

All cultures have recognized the unique value of flowers to communicate feelings. It was a Parisian who penned the first flower dictionary in 1818. Why Madame Charlotte de la Tour decided to decipher the incredible language of flowers is only for us to imagine. Her interpretations rest largely upon plant lore, classical mythology, and love poetry. By the end of the century a book on floriography was a must for any fashionable household.

The language of flowers became most popular during the Victorian Age. It was a time when the rules of etiquette made communication difficult among young men and women. This secret code allowed lovers to convey private messages without alerting the suspicion of their parents, guardians, or chaperones. Intrigues and courtships were carried on with couples barely meeting. Most importantly the language of flowers changed the rules of romance—a shy fellow could catch a maiden's eye, and a pushy suitor could be brushed off.

I cannot meet you tomorrow at 5 o'clock. Be brave, because there is danger of a scandal.

Sweet pea, ivy, oak leaves, lavender, and hemlock.

It is a flower's color that determines much of its romantic meaning. White flowers claim innocence, while red blossoms shout passion. Roses express love, but love in which form? Yellow roses are given to good friends and dark roses are reserved for grief. A pink rose murmurs sweet thoughts

Tulip *I declare my passion.*

"You have set fire to my heart"
The message of this iris is clearest when the yellow "flame" is plain to see.

No doubt misunderstandings often occurred through this secret language as lovers tried to master its complexity. Bouquets required patience to decipher the inherently subtle messages. Even the manner in which a gift was delivered held significance. If the right hand was used to present the flower, the meaning was positive. The advance was rejected if the left hand was used. When the flower was held inverted, the opposite was communicated. No guessing was necessary if the flower was delivered wilted or dead.

Today flowers can be used to communicate messages of love. The next time you find it difficult to express your true feelings, allow the flowers to speak for you. Single flowers can be ordered from florists, and you aren't burdened with the delivery. To ensure that your lover will understand your secret message, include the flower meaning on an unsigned card.

Gardenia *You are pure like this blossom.*

Heliotrope *I adore you. You are the center of my universe.*

Evening Primrose *Humbly I love you.*

Forget-me-not *Think of me while I am away from you.*

Camellia *You have shown much courage.*

White Lily *You are so pure and unsullied.*

Some ingenious lover invented a floral clock so that lovers could plot secret messages giving both the time and nature of the meeting.

Ivy, white campion, and sweet william:
"Meet me tonight at seven"

You could swiftly reply to this interesting bunch by removing the campion and sweet william, and adding lavender, to warn:
"I cannot meet you."

Tiger Lily *I am passionately in love.*

Dog Rose *You are very beautiful.*

Mistletoe *I send you a thousand kisses and blessings.*

Saxifrage *Even a smile from you would reward me.*

When the blindfold of first love falls away, it can either leave true love or disillusionment. In times past, when people got married before they knew very much about their partner, it was all the more important that the language of flowers was fully appreciated during courtship. Subtle signs of a lack of interest had to be heeded.

DISILLUSIONMENT IN LOVE

The code of a less than devoted passion

Bulrush *Please be more discreet.*

Red Geranium *I do not trust you.*

Hydrangea *You are dreadfully fickle.*

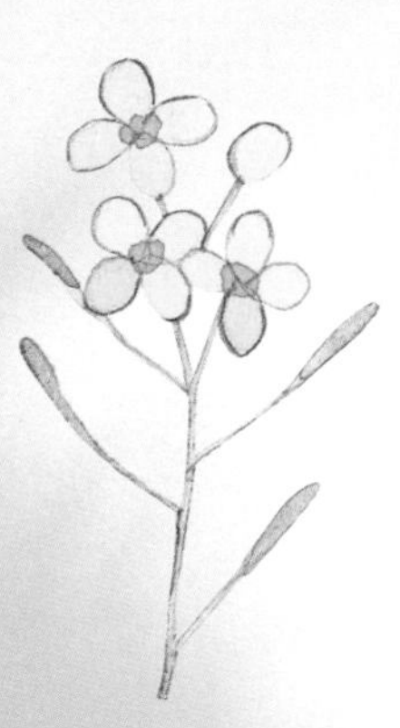

Rocket *You have a rival for my affections.*

French Marigold *Unreasonable jealousy will wreck our relationship.*

White Dahlia *Do not approach me again.*

Nowadays, when love has turned sour, the spurned lover is more at liberty to make a grand, revengeful gesture. But nothing is quite as dignified and poignant as the language of flowers...and it can be a much less hurtful and less humiliating way of getting a very direct message across. For example, a flower as simple as a dandelion can give the very direct message: "Your whole attitude is ridiculous."

Sunflower *You cannot turn my head with ostentation.*

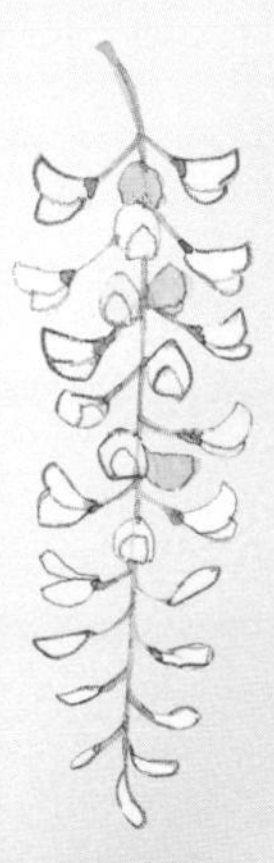

Blue Lobelia *I don't even like you let alone love you.*

Red Poppy *Sudden tactics will fail. Time and patience will win the day.*

Yellow Rose *I love another.*

Laburnum *Why have you neglected me?*

Gladiolus *Your words hurt me very much.*

figures in italics indicate captions

CREDITS

7 top: Nut – Ann Ronan Picture Library
11 bottom: Zodiac – Ann Ronan Picture Library
83 right: Freya – Ann Ronan Picture Library
96 top left: Fatima – Trip / H. Rogers
83 left: Misletoe – Ann Ronan Picture Library
87 top: Wedding – Ann Ronan Picture Library
87 middle left: Myrtle – Trip / H. Rogers
89 left: Hawthorn – Trip / B. Gadsby

My mother once remarked to me that one of my books would outlive me and would come to be considered very beautiful. I did not understand what she meant at the time, but now—looking at *Magic for Lovers*—I feel a sense of comprehension—and pride. Thanks to all those who have made this possible.